SPIRALS of GROWTH

QUEST BOOKS

are published by
The Theosophical Society in America,
a branch of a world organization
dedicated to the promotion of brotherhood and
the encouragement of the study of religion,
philosophy, and science to the end that man may
better understand himself and his place in
the universe. The Society stands for complete
freedom of individual search and belief.
In the Theosophical Classics Series
well-known occult works are made
available in popular editions.

Cover art by *Jane A. Evans*

SPIRALS of GROWTH

The emergence of our "Future-Mind"

Dwight Johnson

This publication made possible with the assistance of the Kern Foundation

The Theosophical Publishing House
Wheaton, Ill. U.S.A.
Madras, India/London, England

For additional information write to:
The Theosophical Publishing House,
306 West Geneva Road, Wheaton, Illinois 60189.
Published by the Theosophical Publishing House,
a department of the Theosophical Society in America.

Library of Congress Cataloging in Publication Data

Johnson, Dwight, 1926-
    Spirals of growth.
    "A Quest book."
    "A Quest original"—Verso of t.p.
    Bibliography: p.
    1. Developmental psychology. 2. Self-actualization
(Psychology) 3. Consciousness. I. Title.
BF713.J63 1983   128   83-70691
ISBN 0-8356-0580-9 (pbk.)

Printed in the United States of America

To Our Teachers

Acknowledgements

This book was made possible by the considerable help at various times of C. Warren Hollister, Michael Win, and Robb Harding. Robb Harding was extremely helpful with the early formulation of these ideas. Professor Hollister has provided generous support at different stages of this undertaking. Elton Hall has been invaluable in refining the entire manuscript, and also by contributing a very thoughtful foreword. This work also owes much to my wife Joyce, in more ways than I can express.

Contents

Foreword

Spirals of Growth is fertile ground for anyone interested in human development. Mr. Johnson reasons that human beings grow through levels of progressive awakening which involve physical, mental, and emotional transitions, each as fundamental as that between infancy and childhood. His essential insights for this work came in 1967 while engaged in graduate studies.

That remarkable year was a watershed for Americans: "flower-children" challenged an establishment which would never be quite the same again. An atmosphere of uncritical freedom and tentative innocence wafted through the nations' major cities, and foreboding signs of communitarian weakness had already gathered on the social horizon. When that brief era—now seen as history—passed, Mr. Johnson sifted through the wreckage for deeper meanings. How could such an upsurge of human spirit become completely diffused, absorbed, and expropriated? How had the wedding of fearless choice and irresponsibility led to pain and conflict? If epochs have coherence in the way individual lives do, what was the significance of the counter-culture? Mr. Johnson decided to bypass traditional history of culture for a psychosocial approach in which individuals, and not events, are the focus of attention. Throughout the 70s he refined his ideas until a comprehensive picture of individual human potential and development emerged.

When Abraham Maslow, the leading light of "third force" psychology, read the basic ideas in 1968 he was enthusiastic about their orientation. Robert Hutchins, America's most humane educational reformer, appreciated their implications. Subsequently, when Erikson, Levinson, Sheehy, Kohlberg and others began to give serious attention to individual life-patterns, the value of Mr. Johnson's broad framework became apparent.

While Erik Erikson has dealt with stages of life largely from a psychological standpoint, Gail Sheehy has boldly described stages of social maturation beyond adulthood, and Lawrence Kohlberg has concerned himself with education and the development of moral sensitivity. But none of these authors has ventured very far into the deceptive landscape of human consciousness, despite the fact that there is ample evidence that consciousness evolves as surely as does the physical body.

There are two reasons for this omission. The obvious reason is the parameters of psychology, sociology, and anthropology. By definition as "social sciences," they are concerned with phenomena, and the processes of consciousness are difficult to observe. Contemporary psychology is not a "science of the soul" as the name suggests, but rather a study of the dynamic structure of the personality. Sociology studies the observable phenomena of group behavior without speculating on the processes of inner development. Anthropology studies the cohesive functions of the human being in a community and discerns the differing valences given to ritual acitivity by different groups, but does not speak of inner processes. The study of consciousness requires both a broader method and a keener discernment.

The second reason for the omission of consciousness is that the languages of intellectual disciplines are inadequate to express development in consciousness, while religious language is too closely tied to specific doctrines to be useful in a nonsectarian perspective. A simple language with new categories had to be generated.

Mr. Johnson's foray into this elusive arena is rightfully tentative. He proposes a model and a perspective on human growth without considering them as absolutes. Drawing upon the words of great modern thinkers who have reflected on their own experiences and activities, and making use of the contributions of researchers in a variety of fields, Mr. Johnson delineates the progressive unfoldment of integrated conscious awareness in individuals. He shows how growth can be stunted at each level, and, most interestingly, how the most mature human beings sustain civilizations and thus influence all of us. He does not presume to know fully the higher reaches of human potentiality, and he shuns the obsessive tendency to judge great minds and categorize them like books on a library shelf. Rather, he shows the pattern of growth in which *every* human being is involved, allowing us to see how the lowliest person and the greatest mind of the age are inseparably linked in a continuum that includes every member of the human race. His perspective allows us to see ourselves in a refreshingly new light that transcends dead dichotomies—success and failure, maturity and immaturity, satisfaction and unhappiness—and makes us participants in a universal Promethean saga. He helps us to see how to insert our personal concerns for growth and fulfillment into the human community.

Mr. Johnson's text is free of psychological and theological jargon and gets to the central issues without becoming bogged down in unnecessary qualifications. This makes his book one we can both learn from and *use*. Furthermore, it gives us good reason to look to the future with hope; and it assures us that the future can hold more significance for us than we might have believed.

Elton A. Hall

Introduction

Exploring the possibilities of the human mind is an exciting and perilous venture. It is also essential. If we hope to subject our increasingly complex world to intelligent, humane direction, if we hope to bring meaning to our own lives, we must understand the processes and potentials of human self-development.

No single field of study can provide us with a comprehensive picture of human development. Indeed, the sciences have dissected man to such a point that his organic wholeness has nearly disappeared from our view. Lecomte du Noüy, in his pioneering book *Human Destiny*, warned that the "scale of observation" affects not only what is known, but what *can be* known. When the scale of observation becomes sufficiently microscopic, one crosses a threshold beyond which it is no longer possible to grasp the original phenomenon. One cannot construct a living organism, for example, solely from the examination of atoms.[1] Nonetheless, recent developments in a variety of fields have disclosed unexpected resources from which it is possible to construct a single coherent theory of human consciousness. This book presents such a theory, drawn from many disciplines—psychology, sociology, philosophy, theology and others—using and juxtaposing elements from each to build a fresh and encompassing framework.

Human consciousness evolves out of relationships between the mind and its environment. The mind, in turn, is an aggregate of processes biologically centered in the brain. Whether or not the mind should be identified with the brain, the potential of man's consciousness is suggested by the prodigious capacity of his cerebral network:

> The average human brain has some 10 billion neurons, or thinking cells, but intelligence rests not so much on the number of cells as on the number of connections between these cells. A neuron can have as many as 10,000 connecting links (dendrites and axons) with other cells or almost none. A single cell can be directly and indirectly linked with as many as 600,000 other cells. These connecting links and the patterns of rhythic cell firing possible through such linkages are what provide the ability to process information. The more the connections, the greater the brain's computational ability.[2]

Brain researchers led by Karl Pribram at Stanford are beginning to consider the brain as a hologram. It would seem that any part of the brain, even a single cell, reflects or encompasses the workings of the entire brain.[3] Still, to cope with functional complexity of this magnitude, the brain employs definite principles of organization. The existence of such principles is exhibited in changes in personal perspective, which might result from absorption in a sunset or an experience of love. Brief or permanent alterations may be brought about by chemical means, including the assimilation of alcohol, psychedelic drugs or opium, by physical or emotional shock, and by internal crises which may achieve the intensity of religious experiences or 'illuminations.' Beyond such examples of altered perspective there are far more basic changes in orientations—changes that define the growth of the human mind. C. G. Jung, for example, suggested that "primordial patterns" and "archetypal forms" guide human growth. Erik Erikson, Jean Piaget, Lawrence Kohlberg and Abraham Maslow among others, have developed theories describing "normal" sequences of growth from infancy through adulthood. Although the physiological basis for these sequences of growth has not been established, it seems likely that if DNA-RNA molecules direct organic development from conception to physical maturity, they are also fundamentally involved in the elusive process of mental growth.

While the qualitative changes from infancy to physical maturity have been widely investigated and are generally understood, remarkably little is known about the sequences of orientations by which an individual can develop beyond socially recognized adulthood. An understanding of the possibilities for postadult development is crucial because growth beyond mere physical maturity is largely dependent upon self-conscious effort. Absence of this understanding gives rise to grim consequences. Individuals who blindly suffer the lonely alienation of an "existential crisis," or the purposelessness that settles like gray fog over middle age, are victims of their failure to understand that their miseries open the possibility of personal growth and deepening awareness. And the effects of their ignorance have more than personal consequences. Our world presents us with bewildering technological challenges to values and human dignity, expanding populations with their demands upon natural resources, and massive political strife. The subtle and penetrating under- standing of highly evolved minds is called for if benevolent purpose is ever to master the sophisticated techniques of modern power. The present analysis endeavors to show how compassionate insight can nur- ture potentials inherent in the future of man.

Beyond these general comments, a few words about the dialectic method supporting this analysis may be helpful. In Hegel's formulation of the classical dialectic, every thesis or proposition gives rise to its own an- tithesis. From the interaction between them a unifying synthesis evolves, only to become, in turn, a new thesis which will initiate the process again. As we resolve old conflicts to reach new integrations, we also create the contradictions that will in time stimulate further change. This process is repeated—each synthesis preserving all previous consolidations—until either a thesis does not give rise to contradiction or the struggle between thesis and antithesis fails. Dialectical analysis can degenerate into mere glib discourse or into deterministic preaching. Still, it has the enormous advantage of illuminating the overall process of change while at the same time allow- ing rigorous descriptive analysis at each stage of development.

There is a clear analogy between a given thesis and each spiral of personal development—child, social adult, individual, etc. Each has a basic center of orienta- tion that provides a coherent pattern of existence, and each spiral can be complete and adequate in itself. But if an individual has the capacity to perceive the limitations (the antithesis) of a particular orientation, that spiral gradually gives way as synthesis takes place. In each case, the ability to perceive and overcome limitations is based upon individual intelligence, sensitivity, and courage. As incompatible perceptions accumulate, dilemmas are uncovered that can be resolved only through a fundamental change in orientation—an ascent to the next spiral. Thus it is difficult for a child to resist growth—no matter how satisfactory the family experience—because as maturation occurs childhood orientation gives rise to contradictions and limitations. The transition to a new spiral of growth is accompanied by a normative crisis, adolescence for example, where perceptions are reorganized to embrace new environmental realities and expanded awareness. The word *transition* is used throughout this analysis to describe an unanchored period of time in which the evolving mind synthesizes a more comprehensive center of orientation. Each reorientation processes information in new ways and develops new ways of interacting with a larger whole. Rather than a static term like *stage*, the word *spiral* was chosen to project the idea of a continuity that coils in one plane—like a watch spring—around one particular center or orientation, until the accumulation of discordant perceptions opens the way to personal growth. Thus, thesis and antithesis give way to synthesis in a higher spiral.

Organic coherence underlies the variety and confusion of human behavior. Whatever the details, men are embraced by a common genetic potential. Expressed through human consciousness, that potential can awaken a deeper and more comprehensive engagement with evolving life, and therefore with itself. As a contribution to such an awakening, this book will explore the conditions underlying personal growth in the Western world.

Spiral I

The Infant

Any starting point for a study of human development is at best arbitrary. Even before conception there are the complexities of a vast "genetic pool" that resolve into the delicate protein structures of sperm and egg. From fertilization to birth, momentous struggles and changes occur, each molding the future of the individual and even the future of life on earth. Then there is the great trauma of birth itself, a throbbing balance of enzymes and hormones, physical force and helping hands, pain and excitement which culminate in the first breath of a human being. This analysis will not concentrate upon prenatal transformations: it will commence with a study of infancy, the two-year period following birth where the definition of self and the struggle for meaning begins.

Infancy is widely understood to evolve through a complex interplay between sensory activity and environmental conditions as the infant nurses, strengthens muscles, struggles to crawl and walk, and begins to convert noise into symbolic language. Each phase is undeniably important as a firm basis for further growth, and each has received massive study from child development specialists. But reviewing all the intricacies of infant adaptation and growth is not necessary to establish the framework that renders infancy comprehensible as the first major stage in human life.

The infant center of orientation is clearly the mother or maternal person who nurtures the baby and attends to his needs.* The mother provides a secure base of knowing from which the infant can venture out to assimilate the unknown. Sigmund Freud described infancy as an "oral" stage where "impulses" such as sucking enable the baby to interact with his mother as a source of nourishment and emotional well-being. The importance of the infant-mother relationship has been characterized by the child psychologist Erik Erikson in terms of trust:

> The psychiatrists, obstetricians, pediatricians, and anthropologists, to whom I feel closest, today would agree that the firm establishment of enduring patterns for the balance of basic trust over mistrust is the first task of the budding personality and therefore first of all a task for maternal care....Mothers create a sense of basic trust in their children by that kind of administration which in its quality combines sensitive care of the baby's individual needs and a firm sense of personal trustworthiness with the trusted framework of their communities' life style.[1]

This statement discloses the widely held agreement among specialists on the importance of the maternal relationship, and it also indicates that Erikson's analytic approach is focused upon human adaptation to society.

---

*Masculine adjectives (he, him, his) are used for convenience of expression but should be understood to include girls or women as well.

The phrase "enduring patterns for the balance of basic trust over mistrust" is the basis of a theory about healthy adaptation to society in a potentially chaotic and hostile world. Complementing Erikson's approach, the Swiss psychologist Jean Piaget has examined intellectual development to describe the first two years of human growth as a "sensori-motor" phase because the infant is stimulated by his senses but is dependent upon his body—not symbols or thought—for self-expression. For Piaget, the mother is the audience for communication because she responds to the infant's needs.

Unless one is a strict behaviorist like B. F. Skinner, one cannot say that symbolic thought is not active in the infant, but only that it is not observed at this stage. The one exception is infant linguistic development, although the level of symbolic thought involved in infant speech is also subject to controversy, in part because the degree to which essential linguistic activities are innate is not clear. Noam Chomsky's work in syntactic structures and "deep grammar" is suggestive but inconclusive.

Erikson's concern with the development of a "healthy personality" in Western society and Piaget's interest in intellectual growth are only two of many theoretical approaches that stress the importance of infant-mother orientation during the first years of life. But since our concern in discussing the first two spirals of growth is merely to sketch out the steps that provide a basis for adult development, the theories of Erikson and Piaget will serve as an ample foundation.

Infant-Child Transition

The sense of autonomy that the infant develops through physical growth gradually erodes the exclusivity of the infant-mother relationship. Walking and talking, for example, allow the child to explore possibilities outside the realm of the mother, while infant mobility makes constant maternal care impossible. Thus the difficult transition to childhood begins, characterized by Dr. Benjamin Spock as "terrible two," when the infant-mother relationship no longer satisfies the needs of the growing child.

Freud terms the period from approximately two to four years the "anal" stage because a growing infant is stubbornly caught between contradictory modes of behavior patterned after a "retention-elimination" struggle to control the bowels. Erikson follows Freudian theory to call this period a time of crisis wherein "muscular maturation sets the stage for experimentation with two simultaneous sets of social modalities—*holding on* and *letting go*."[2] The struggle is normally resolved as the child gains a "sense of autonomy" ("self-control without loss of self-esteem") under the guidance of firm and understanding parents. The same normative crisis is analyzed by Piaget as a "preconceptual phase" in which the growing infant makes fumbling attempts to grasp the strange new world of symbols beyond sensori-motor communication.[3] Symbols have only a subjective meaning during this phase, for the child cannot grasp the symbolic intricacies of adult thought. Intelligence grows as the child moves from the known to that which is unknown, and assimilates it into the known.

The general framework for resolving the frustrations that accompany growing autonomy was established by Freud. As he explained, the child learns that it must inevitably go without immediate satisfaction, postpone gratification, learn to endure a degree of pain, and renounce certain sources of pleasure. Thus the child becomes "reasonable," is no longer wholly controlled by the "pleasure principle," but begins to follow the "reality principle." The reality principle also seeks pleasure, but it is a delayed and possibly diminished pleasure, within the possibilities of external "reality."

Since the family is the heart of environmental "reality" in early childhood, a sense of autonomy within a family concludes the infant-child transition.

The Child

During the second spiral of growth the child develops, within the structured environment of family life, the capacity for adaptation to a larger society and his own future. Although the child's world soon expands in a widening network of relationships, the home and family normally remain the focus for security and action until adolescence leads to concentration upon the possibilities of the extrafamilial social world. The centrality of the family in childhood orientation was emphasized by Erikson when he stated: "The fate of childhood identification depends on the child's satisfactory interaction with a trustworthy and meaningful hierarchy of roles as provided by the generations living together in some form of family."[1]

For Erikson, the first step in child-family relationships is identification with parents:

> Having found a firm solution of his problem of autonomy, the child of four and five is faced with the next step—and with the next crisis. Being firmly convinced that he is a person, the child must now

> find out what kind of person he is going to be. And
> here he hitches his wagon to nothing less than a star:
> he wants to be like his parents, who to him appear
> very powerful and very beautiful, although quite
> unreasonably dangerous. He "identifies with them,"
> he plays with the idea of how it would be to be
> them.[2]

In imitating his parents, he evokes the ability to distinguish right from wrong within the structure of family life. This ability enables the child to develop a "sense of initiative" because he can now make responsible decisions on his own. The developing moral sense is critical for self-definition since it passes beyond crude categorizations of right and wrong into better and worse, preferable (for some end) and undesirable, beautiful and ugly, good enough and unsatisfactory—that is, into the fine shades of ethical and esthetic texture that eventually make of each life a unique tapestry instead of just broadcloth. Once the child can initiate activity which in itself is a potent form of choice, he is ready to develop the capacity to bring a decision to productive completion. Erikson calls this capacity a "sense of industry" where the child from seven through twelve wins recognition as "he develops the pleasure of work completion by steady attention and persevering diligence."[3]

Piaget's examination of intellectual development parallels Erikson's sequence of adaptation to Western society. Age four to seven is described as a "phase of intuitive thought," because a child can think with symbols but still does not understand their interrelated complexity in the world of adult thought. Hence the thought process in this phase is largely subjective or intuitive. Symbolic interrelationships are gradually absorbed as the child asks seemingly endless series of questions

until awareness of rudimentary patterns brings him
to the threshold of rational or nonintuitive thought.
This awareness introduces Piaget's "phase of concrete
operations" around age seven. Gradually, the child
shifts from inductive to deductive thinking as he learns
to generalize and deduce relationships from simple experiences. By twelve the child has developed the capacity to coordinate this personal experience with the
physical and social world around him.

Piaget and his colleagues have found that critical
changes in moral outlook accompany intellectual
development. Around age seven children move from
judging an act as bad in terms of mainly physical consequences, to bad in terms of the intent to do harm; from
viewing an act as either right or wrong, to an awareness
of diversity in views of right or wrong; from saying an
act is bad because it elicits punishment, to saying an act
is bad because it violates a rule; and from advocating
severe and painful punishment after stories of misdeeds,
to favoring milder punishment leading to restitution to
the victim and reform of the culprit. It would seem that
much of what it means to be human in terms of higher
sensibilities begins around age seven.

More recent research by Lawrence Kohlberg has
refined moral development into three major levels with
six types of moral judgement:

Level I.	Premoral	
Type 1.		Punishment and obedience orientation
Type 2.		Naive instrumental hedonism
Level II.	Morality of conventional Role-Conformity	
Type 3.		Good-boy morality of maintaining good relations, approval by others
Type 4.		Authority maintaining morality

Level III.   Morality of Self-Accepted Moral
             Principles
    Type 5.   Morality of contract, of individual
                 rights, and of democratically
                 accepted law
    Type 6.   Morality of individual principles
                 of conscience[4]

As explained by Kohlberg, the premoral level decreases
with age while role-conformity increases until age
thirteen and then stabilizes. Self-accepted morality continues to increase from age thirteen to sixteen as the
child moves into adolescence. These levels of moral
development are products of the child's efforts to make
sense out of experience in a complex societal environment, with each level arising sequentially from its
predecessors:

> Evidence suggests that the use of a more advanced
> stage of thought depends upon earlier attainment
> of each preceding stage and that each involves a
> restructuring and displacement of previous stages of
> thought.[5]

This general conclusion parallels the findings of Erikson.
These stages of development are not simply sequential:
they are dependent upon preceding stages. They *evolve.*
We will see that sequential development with restructuring and displacement of previous stages is the pattern
for all spirals of growth.

The work of Piaget and Kohlberg offers an admirable
basis for understanding how the family encourages
childhood mental and moral development. It serves as a
constant and reliable audience while offering feedback
within a context of love and reassurance. Thus the family provides the child with a stable center of orientation
for learning the complexities of symbolic thought and
moral judgment. In the family are also engendered the

emotional and rational notions that the child carries into adulthood. At best, these notions are rooted in an awareness of cultural continuity that integrates past and present, art and technology, ideals and concrete examples, and above all a sense of environmental continuity that includes rocks, spiders, rabbits and stars as harmonious with the world of man.

This brief sketch of the ideas of Erikson, Piaget and Kohlberg only suggests the subtlety and depth of their thought. It does not pretend to do justice to the rich variety of present knowledge concerning human development during infancy and childhood. Yet one implication is obvious: the family unit can aid or damage the development of human potential at any of the phases listed above. Whether the basic unit living together as a family includes several generations, has a matriarchal or patriarchal structure, or consists of broad community as in, for instance, an Israeli kibbutz, it must be characterized by reliability, intimacy, decisiveness of relationships, and firm bonds with the surrounding society. The absence of such qualities forbodes serious problems in later life.

Sociologists and psychologists have observed that the family trend in Western society is toward increasingly small, rootless units with working-mother/absent-father living patterns, often prone to accepting divorce as an alternative to problem solving rather than as a last resort. These families frequently cannot supply the stability and supervision necessary for healthy child development. Perhaps more important, the efforts of warm and understanding parents can be diluted by outside pressures encountered in school and peer groups, television and other mass media, the treatment of children as an economic market, and divided loyalties through divorce.

The cumulative effect of these social forces is growing disintegration of the child center of orientation. A child can imitate adults other than his parents or win recognition outside the home; he can be encouraged by specialists to express himself or be taught rational thinking by teachers. But the small familial environment is important in discouraging the tendency to escape conflict situations. The "mass society" with its lack of continuity allows individuals to flee every hard social choice and potential conflict, but at the price of diminishing the potentials of growth. A sense of identity, responsibility, and purpose within a small environment cannot be formed without a stable child-family relationship to center the process of growth. When this relationship is missing, the result is alienated, dissatisfied adults who are out of step with the "normal" sequence of growth inherited by humanity. Just as the infant must develop what Erikson calls a "sense of basic trust" in the mother to form "the cornerstone of a healthy personality," the child must develop the capacity for adulthood within a warm and stable family environment. Otherwise there is little basis for the subsequent growth that fulfills the possibilities of the human mind.

Child-Social Adult Transition

Limitations in Spiral II orientation arise when the approach of physical maturity combines with expanding social interaction to overwhelm the narrowness of family life. As new and more inclusive vistas unfold, the identity established within a family is gradually recast within the broader and more rewarding framework of society. Society is meant here in a sociological sense that includes community, locality, class, ethnic tradition, or that social environment which governs individual norms, codes, values and sentiments.

Freud described adolescence as a period of intense conflict with divided loyalties, contradictory aspirations, erratic behavior, and unrestrained enthusiasm. Conflict is resolved when the father-figure authority and family dominance are replaced by a social superego. Though differing in their analyses, Alfred Adler, Karen Horney, Erich Fromm, Abraham Maslow and others rejected Freud's tendency to attribute adolescent and adult problems (neuroses) to early childhood trauma and to cast them in terms of sexual development. Nevertheless, there is little dissension from the general proposition that earlier growth experiences, both positive and negative, profoundly influence the actualization of growth potentials in later life.

Extending the structure of Freudian theory, Erikson has produced a very thorough analysis of adolescence. Age thirteen to twenty is described as a "psychosocial moratorium" with seven distinct dimensions of social adaptation through which an adolescent finds a "sense of identity" within his society. As an example, one of these dimensions is "leadership polarization" where the youth experiments with the abilities to lead and to follow in various social activities.

For Jean Piaget adolescence introduces a "phase of formal operations" wherein the ability to think deductively (through childhood "concrete operations") is incorporated within the structure of adult thought and emotional expression. As outlined in Spiral II, moral development continues into Level III of Kohlberg's categories: the "Morality of Self-Accepted Moral Principles." Thus mental and emotional activities become more powerful and useful by internalizing the patterns of adult mental and moral activity. A youth arrives at the threshold of intellectual and moral maturity around age fourteen or fifteen when he is able to depend solely upon socially accepted patterns of judgment and thought.

As understood by Erikson, Piaget and Kohlberg, adolescence is the period when a youth develops the skills and moral outlook necessary to become a capable adult within his society. In traditional or non-technological societies, the transition to adulthood is usually brief and relatively smooth. The skills and value systems are clearly defined and easily learned during childhood and the brief period of intense apprenticeship that accompanies puberty. Children are given myths, images, stories and symbols that are noble and elevating. These become living presences that help to emancipate them from the clutches of adolescence. Moreover, most of the living arrangements are determined by birth or are contrived. By fourteen or fifteen a "sense of identity" within the society is complete, and intellectual/moral maturity reaches full adult status.

But transition to adulthood becomes more difficult when the segment of society entered by a youth is so complex that more time is required to absorb adult skills, as in the case of an aristocracy, or when social norms and roles are profoundly disrupted. Wars, sweeping technological changes, or revolutionary upheavals, for example, can disrupt the commonly accepted passage to adulthood. The modern adolescent faces another serious problem. In addition to the complexity of adult skills and the frequency of cultural shocks like war and economic uncertainty, the reservoir of social norms and values sanctioned by the local community has become ill-defined. Learning to be a capable and responsible adult is now a very difficult process.

Thinkers as diverse as Margaret Mead and Mircea Eliade believe that the turbulent adolescent of Western industrialized societies is largely a product of the collapse of definitive social norms which confront the adolescent through widely recognized social rituals such as coming-of-age ceremonies. Eric von Ganepp's *Rites of Passage* remains a valuable study of the critical functions of collective participation in an individual's transition from one socially recognized level of development to another.

Trapped in a long and awkward period of adjustment while overwhelmed by newly awakened physiological powers and passions, the modern adolescent faces what Erikson describes as "defense against the sense of identity diffusion." To preserve a sense of identity "adolescents help one another temporarily through such discomfort by forming cliques and by stereotyping themselves, their ideals, and their enemies."[6] Hence the phenomenon of the "teenager," replete with hero identification, elaborate ego fantasies, raging fads, passionate but ephemeral loyalties, and a bewildering variety of behavioral rebellions—all, in more or less extreme forms. These are elements of a prolonged normative crisis which accompanies the child-adult transition in Western society.

Since adolescence is a time where preparation is made for capable adulthood, a long transition is sometimes apparent. But when the transition is too lengthy, prolonged anxiety creates serious personal and social problems that limit the human potential for adaptability and growth.

As mentioned in Spiral II, the child center of orientation is breaking down due to problems within and outside the family. This breakdown forces young people to participate in complex social situations without the sense of stability provided by identity emerging within the family unit. Slum children, forced to live in the streets without adult support or guidance, begin to exhibit "teenage behavior" as early as five or six years of age. With the breakdown of the family, children in all classes of society are now sharing adolescent characteristics as "teenagers" become younger and younger. In addition, commensurate with this psychological foreshadowing of adolescence in childhood years, earlier puberty has been observed in America and some other Western societies. Attributing this curious phenomenon to enhanced diet hardly seems to provide a complete explanation.

The "teenage" phenomenon is also found in older and older individuals. Again, this is best seen in the slums where the prospect of adulthood holds so little promise. If being an adult means economic drudgery or purposeless employment, if marriage is ephemeral and citizenship meaningless, there is little incentive to assume adult identity. Since teenagers have "never had it so good" and adulthood is seen as a colorless bog, many young people play the "adult game" merely to obtain the financial resources necessary to prolong adolescence.

Rejection of adult identity is often reinforced by the disillusionment that follows the youthful tendency to idealize the world. This process is compounded by the fact that young people are no longer ignorant about the modern world, due to knowledge of political and social events absorbed since early childhood through television and other media.[7] Ideals of human dignity, justice, and peace juxtaposed against such social realities as exploitation, prejudice, and hypocrisy generate tensions leading to disillusionment. It seems reasonable to add that disillusionment with the adult world is nearly inevitable if a young person's idealism faces his sophisticated knowledge of contemporary events without a balancing understanding of our distressful human heritage, the background which engendered the present crisis. The pressure of mass media would seem to call for young people to gain a much more thorough appreciation of the devastating challenges and groping responses by which the human enterprise has managed to evolve.

While the child-adult transition is beginning earlier and ending later, the process of social identification that traditionally resolved it is breaking down. Erikson points out that adult identity formation has two dimensions: "the selective repudiation and mutual assimilation of childhood identifications" by the adolescent, combined with "the process by which a society (often through subsocieties) identifies the young individual."[8] Thus, the adolescent must break his childhood identification while society recognizes his new adult status. Within this statement is the implication that social institutions—marriage, apprenticeship, church, schools, and military service—are meeting points between the adolescent and his society where adult identity can form.

Even two generations ago this arrangement worked reasonably well. From the youth's point of view, institutions were the road to acceptance as a capable adult: the "psychosocial moratorium" was filled with training and help; marriage engendered family and community responsibility; and military service could literally "make a man out of you." From society's viewpoint, institutional arrangements were a means of controlling undesirable behavior and creating responsible citizens. Local schools had punitive powers, failure at apprenticeship brought economic peril, powerful community pressure could be applied through the institution of marriage, and dishonorable discharge brought disgrace to a whole family.

With the prevailing disintegration of the community ties that made sanctions intimately meaningful to both the youth and his local society, repudiating childhood identifications corresponds less and less to acceptance as an adult through social institutions. Rather, events are moving in the opposite direction. As the adolescent becomes an adult, it is he who frequently identifies society with feelings of hostility and bitterness. In other words, the institutional commitments that were once effective ways to form responsible adult identity have become the means through which some young adults have grown cynical and disgusted with their social environment. The following examples should help to make this point clear.

When the adolescent need to defray "identity diffusion" combines with the transitional tendency to find "completeness" through another, there is a great sense of compatibility and shared values that frequently leads to marriage. The young couple then strikes out on its own, but in modern society the partners rarely find or develop the deep community attachments that provide a secure framework for the extension of family life. Moreover, as Erikson indicates:

> Earlier crystallizations of identity can become subject to renewed conflict, when changes in the quality and quantity of drive, expansions of mental equipment, and new and often conflicting social demands all make previous adjustments appear insufficient, and, in fact, make previous opportunities and rewards suspect.[9]

Compatibility and shared values can prove illusory when adult identity is crystallized, and young people find they are living with strangers or even enemies. In the absence of secure communal ties that encourage and aid readjustment, the result is frequently divorce. The one area where society does enter the picture is through the process of divorce; but society treats collapsing marriages as legal and statistical rather than human problems. The expense, technical lies, and formal indifference of the divorce procedures provoke disgust and cynicism. Marriage, once one of the most powerful institutions for including young people in society, has become increasingly nonsocial in character, as well as a source of hostility toward society. Rather than marriage functioning as the entree into wider social participation, married couples may see themselves as standing against the world.

A similar example of disintegration of positive social identification is evident in massive institutions such as those of higher education. As the personal concern that once justified local community control of the content and moral tone of its schools gives way, educational aims have necessarily centered on individual self-realization and fulfillment; the student prepares for his own future rather than that of his nonexistent community. This process would appear to represent consummation of the old republican and democratic dream that the purpose of society was to help each person fulfill his maximum potential, that fulfillment allowing him to best serve society as a whole. But higher education frequently thwarts ·self-realization while frustrating preparation for the future. On one side, self-exploration is blocked by endless rules and requirements, many of them carry-overs from the period when local society was directly involved with each student. On the other hand, universities have not established participatory communities to replace the local communities which provided a secure framework for transition to responsible adulthood. To many students, the main emphasis in large universities appears to center on the mechanical process of training them to pass examinations. This trend can be discerned in the tendency of institutions to advertise their success in terms of number of students graduated and degrees granted. This is quantification of education with a vengeance. In reaction, many students become cynical and some revolt. Such reactions may indicate that the student is becoming an adult, but an adult disgusted with the institutions of higher learning and frequently hostile to the society that sustains them.

The process by which for thousands of years people have become integrated with society is undergoing a basic change. In response, millions throughout the world are groping for answers to the massive challenge presented by the collapse of fixed localism and an extended child-adult transition. From theologians and sociologists to city planners and social workers, individuals concerned with the convolutions of modern society should find nothing new in the trends described above. However, they may benefit from this brief overview which coordinates the social transformations around us with the possibilities of the human mind.

In considering human possibilities in a rapidly changing world, it is apparent that the sequence of normal human growth cannot be ignored or rejected: countless years of biological and social development are not to be instantly displaced, if they can be displaced at all. The mother/parents/basic family/extended family/local community progression has long been fundamental to the human condition, and it forms the firm foundation for further adaptation and growth. While recognizing that the specific cast of each step is highly variable, to prolong or circumvent the sequence as a whole is to risk

the effects of sweeping alienation, corrupted idealism,
and cynical hosility toward society. It is to leave the
young severed from the source of their strength for the
challenges ahead.

The Social Adult

This spiral marks the beginning of adulthood. It is termed the social adult spiral of growth because social values augmented by social sensitivity provide the center of orientation. Through childhood and adolescence the social adult has been attuned to the prevailing norms, values, codes and sentiments that surround him. Hence, he wants to do "what's right" within the framework of his society or subsociety; and this desire, combined with the technical skills mastered through long preparation, enable him to be a responsible and capable member of his particular society or subculture. The mentality of most adults has long centered in the stolid reliability of Spiral III to provide the sustained group coherence that made civilization possible.

Erikson holds that adult identity "must be based on an implicit mutual contract between the individual and society," and "identity formation neither begins nor ends with adolescence: it is a life-long development largely unconscious to the individual and his society."[1] While the phrase "implicit mutual contract" may have a peculiar ring, the general idea is clear. Intimate contacts within a family make the welfare of each member dependent upon the others. Family relations become a source of misery and frustration when mutual duties and obligations are not discharged. Hence the duties and obligations owed among members of a family produce childhood patterns of responsibility and sensitivity to the expectations of others. Once an adult becomes responsible for the well-being of his own family, he must then increase his knowledge of accepted patterns of action and thought and expand his sensitivity to others. Otherwise, ignorance or insensitivity will produce unhappiness for his whole family and social constellation.

Internalization of social values is more readily explored than social sensitivity. This is because the value patterns must be communicated and widely understood before they can be internalized by members of a society. As a society grows larger, the patterns become simplified so that they can be understood by a variety of people in a variety of contexts. From the subtle value frameworks found in small primitive societies, value patterns become increasingly simplified in larger societies until they come to rest in the readily understandable polarities that pervade the large societies of our modern world. Thus the dichotomous thought and behavior of modern adults is rooted in widely accepted polarities: good or bad, friend or enemy, we or they, work or leisure, success or failure, etc. The specific content carried by such value patterns—what is good or what constitutes failure—will vary within each society or subculture. Nevertheless, acceptability is the hallmark of social adult thinking, and divergent points of view are seen as either antisocial or irrelevant.

Since dualistic categories are the lowest common denominator for the internalization of the formulas that bind men together as members of a society, considerable thought has been given to the psychological basis behind them. Polarity is generally understood as the reflection of a fundamental tension deep within man —as described in the body-soul, devil-God, darkness-light religious formulas. Freud analyzed the roots of dualism in terms of an "id-ego" or "pleasure principle" in tension with the "ego-superego" or "reality principle." Along Freudian lines the basic dualistic framework can be described more simply as tension between the emotions and the intellect. Thus the emotions demand complete absorption in experience while the intellect strives to maintain order by channeling emotional demands into acceptable patterns of behavior. The balance between emotions and intellect is, of course, in a state of constant flux. But in general, when the accent falls on the emotions, behavioral patterns can run the gamut from raw emotional outpourings to sexual promiscuity to violence; or if the accent is on intellect, the tendency is toward rigid adherence to order, rules and tradition.

While refined aspects of the tension between emotions and intellect can be seen in subsequent spirals of growth, the dualistic mentality is most clearly reflected in Spiral III, where dualism is simply accepted and incorporated as an unconscious basis for action and thought. Even though the social adult becomes adept in the shifting subleties of hobbies or business activities, he remains fixed in Spiral III as long as black-or-white formulas dominate his life. If a particular adult begins to explore the ambiguity of his black-or-white attitudes, growth beyond social adulthood has begun. Polarity is not intrinsically antithetical to growth, but resistance to recognizing ambiguities in polarized categories is. The growth-oriented individual is at least stimulated, and perhaps excited, by this challenge of ambiguity. The individual who fears growth (going back in some cases as far as the original infant encounter with the need to trust) will shun ambiguity and even deny it. This is the source of the common belief that the greatest fanatic is secretly the greatest doubter. Eric Hoffer investigated this phenomenon in *The True Believer*.

The process whereby social sensitivity augments the internalization of social values presents subjective problems which are difficult to resolve. Sensitivity toward others, as expressed by terms like empathy, sympathy and human warmth, has remained tenaciously aloof from causative analysis. There is, however, some evidence that this capacity is not simply an accident of birth. Work in the area of "sensitivity training" indicates that sensitivity toward others is rooted in spontaneous environmental awareness. This training rests on the belief that if a child or adult is encouraged to be continuously aware of his environment, of the pebbles underfoot and the colors of rooms, he will develop a spontaneous sensitivity to his whole environment, including other people. Eventually, his human relationships will be based on spontaneous awareness of the emotions, attitudes and mannerisms of those he meets. One might say as a very general rule, that sensitivity to others and to one's surroundings is inversely proportionate to one's self-concern; that is, sensitivity presupposes, not delicacy or fraility, but rather self-confidence and self-knowledge.

Although sensitivity toward others has positive connotations, it can as readily become the basis for duplicity as for compassion. Spiral III sensitivity, however, normally serves as an unconscious guide for the internalization and utilization of social values, rather than a conscious basis for manipulating others. Above all, social sensitivity ripens the possibilities for human interaction, thereby providing a sound foundation for expansion into more evolved spirals of growth.

The panorama of social adulthood displays a variety of differences among individuals. These hinge upon the content of the value formulas internalized, the degree of social sensitivity, the kaleidoscopic facts of personal experience, the areas where thought breaks through black-or-white dualities, and individual emphasis on either emotions or intellect. But the common anchorage in social orientation leads to the possibility of observations and comments about social adults in general and the adequacy of social arrangements for them. Hence Freud's comment is relevant here; when asked to describe a healthy foundation for adult life, he replied with beautiful simplicity, "to love and to work."

Similar dictums have been advanced as guidelines for the content of value formulas throughout the ages: faith, hope and charity—do unto others—eat, drink and be merry—are common examples of advice offered as foundations for adult life. Yet Freud's comment has a peculiar significance for the present. Erikson indicates that Freud meant love as both the expansion of generosity and of genital love, and work as productivity that would not overwhelm the capacity to be sexual and loving. While Erikson's explanation is sound within the framework of psychoanalysis, the connotations of love and work have profoundly changed since Freud made this statement.

Adult love has traditionally centered around the stability and continuity of family life. But family love and life have recently been weakened by the acceptability and frequency of divorce combined with widespread sexual freedom. Even children—both a focus for the expression of love and a means for continuing social involvement—have become a source of bewilderment and frustration. Not only do children frequently scatter, leaving parents with empty houses in decaying neighborhoods; they also tend to internalize value systems entirely different from those of their parents. In fact, the rapidity with which closely allied generations of social adults can internalize antipathetic values is one of the most striking aspects of the modern world. It could be argued that children internalize the values their parents exhibited in practice and not what their parents give lip service to. This line of reasoning suggests that as social norms become increasingly confused, the gap between theory and practice tends to widen, with unanticipated and often unfortunate consequences in the family. In any case love, as centered in the family, is less and less a stable foundation for adult life.

Since Marx, the erosion of traditional values attached to work has received considerable attention under the category of "work alienation." In addition to alienation, simple work security has been crumbling under the impact of automation and cybernation. From the opposite side, shorter working hours, increased buying power, and the prospect of retirement mean that more time and energy are now devoted to nonwork activities. In sum, the possibility of building a healthy adult life on traditional work values is increasingly unlikely.

While the traditional foundations of love and work are giving way, they are only two examples from a multitude of problems generated by rapid and continual change. The content of almost every dualistic perspective has been subjected to alteration as yesterday's enemies become today's friends, and yesterday's social virtues, such as large families, become a source of economic peril. There has been an accompanying avalanche of ideas, which, since the Renaissance, have insisted that human merit is attained through self-assertion. Unfortunately, self-assertion is frequently contrary to the nonassertive values most congenial to the social adult mentality. The social adult wants to do what is right within his society. Among the most recent ideas are judgments by social critics like David Reisman who insist that "other-directed" adults provide the substance for repressive manipulation and stifling conformity. Rapid change capped by an avalanche of ideas has almost buried the stolid reliability inherent in dualistic perspectives.

Besieged from all sides, the lives of people in their numerically dominant spiral of growth settle into patterns of futility or desperation. In the absence of reliable values, they turn to material goods and popular fashions, seeking self-respect as an individual from minute differences in products and styles essentially the same. Certain events, like the World Series, become extremely important because they represent some semblance of shared continuity with the past. Perhaps television's glow most clearly illuminates their "other-directed" refuge in widely shared isolation. Perhaps it only reflects a desire to participate coupled with a wish to escape responsibility, resulting in a kind of social voyeurism.

Before considering a more positive approach to adult life in the modern world, it is necessary to examine a possible source of confusion about the behavior of social adults. As previously discussed, normal adult identity is dependent upon "the child's satisfactory interaction with a trustworthy and meaningful hierarchy of roles as provided by the generations living together in some sort of family." When this is not provided through intimate family interactions, the child often matures without internalizing a sense of responsibility or sensitivity to the expectations of others. The result is an infantile adult who is alienated from the source of his identity as a social adult because he has not internalized the child center of orientation. He therefore tends to be insensitive to others, nonresponsible, and confused about socially accepted patterns of behavior. If he has attained the intellectual maturity described by Piaget, he can manage a semblance of adult behavior when life is smooth and untroubled; but when placed under severe stress he reverts to the security of mother or early parental orientations. In pursuing the warmth of infancy or early childhood, the infant-adult may turn to alcohol, drugs, a mother or father substitute as a sexual partner, or a domineering political messiah. When attempts to find warmth and security are unsuccessful, anxiety and frustration are expressed in wild emotional displays, capricious violence, or behavioral excesses reminiscent of the infant-child transition.[2]

Increasing numbers of infantile adults can distort norms of maturity statistically generated in behaviorist empirical psychology. The infantile-adult can be encouraged to grow into full adulthood through individual, group, or community therapy, but the response to his problems is substantially different from that which is necessary to alleviate the plight of the social adult. The social adult is not so much the victim of circumstances in his life but of a sweeping metamorphosis in the structure of human society, where his values and position have been buried by the size and complexity, the speed and power, the mobility and technology of massive social change. These qualities of social change are not in themselves necessarily detrimental, but they become so when size is ungoverned, complexity is random, speed undirected, power unchanneled, mobility without purpose and technology unplanned. Unfortunately, in industrial and postindustrial societies, social forethought and community ends are commonly ignored with devastating effects on individuals.

The truest measure for the identity of man in general is Spiral III consciousness. This is not only because social adults represent the majority of people in most industrial societies, but because the dualistic structure of their action and thought reflects the condition of man's evolutionary relationship to his environment. Therefore the possibility of creating a viably humane world rests heavily upon an appreciation and understanding of Spiral III consciousness, upon its limitations, strengths, and position in the panorama of human consciousness.

Because the social adult is both limited by the rigidity of a dichotomizing perspective and susceptible to manipulation, both characteristics require further consideration, for they are sources of strength as well as weakness, and they are closely interwoven. Bound by the rigid dimensions of black-or-white polarities in response to environmental challenge and change, social adult action and thought are governed by the content of dualistic formulas. If the content is adequate to the challenges faced by an adult and his society, the result can be benevolent social stability; but if the content is inadequate, then confusion, repression, or violence can result. In the modern world, the values provided by religious and social philosophies have either collapsed or are undergoing a process of transformation. The absence of adequate value frameworks, together with the demise of local communities, have placed the social adult in a position where he is victimized by those who command the techniques of organization and control. When a man is no longer certain of what is right or wrong, or even who or what he is in relation to others, he can only turn to "specialists" for instruction about

"what's right" in his society. The social adult is therefore particularly subject to manipulation and coercion
when the content of dualistic values is inadequate to
environmental challenge and change.

A substantial part of any resolution of this problem
lies in creating overall value frameworks that are adequate to the conditions imposed by an increasingly
interdependent and challenging world. Since this
Herculean task is the responsibility of higher spirals of
consciousness, the process through which adequate
values are developed and projected into history will be
considered as spirals unfold. One can anticipate,
however, that the solution must involve a willingness to
be guided and governed by the wise rather than the
powerful and prestigious.

When the social adult is secure from confusion about
"what's right," his inherent strength emerges. The solidity of dualistic perspective can provide endurance in the
face of adversity, a strength that is more than capable of
resisting manipulation by more subtle minds. Even more
important is the capacity of the social adult to relate to
others, for the desire to do "what's right" is the basis for
accommodation and cooperation among humans.

Social Adult—Individual Transition

The social adult world may be endlessly busy and absorbing, but behind the activity generated by social
consciousness is the pull toward self-consciousness or
individuality. At the roots of what individuality has
grown to mean in Western society are the great Homeric
legends that inspired men with the idea that they could
transcend the gods or nature to determine their own
fate. For almost three thousand years the crafty and

resourceful Ulysses has beckoned human endeavor into realms where men must master adversity in order to survive and grow beyond themselves. Even Heracles, driven mad by Hera, could free Prometheus and win immortality.

Precisely why some heed the call to grow beyond Spiral III while others refuse lies deep in the interplay between capacity and opportunity, courage and encouragement, seductive habitude and perilous adventure. All social adults probably flirt with choice, occasionally tempt the fates, and have their Cinderella fantasies, but only a few are willing to face the risks and perils encountered in the plunge from relative security into unfamiliar lands. At some point one cannot help asking oneself "Who am I?" and "What do I really want?" As stated by E. F. Schumacher, insightful commentator on modern problems:

> All the time, there exists, however, the possibility that I may take the matter in hand and quite freely and deliberately *direct* my attention to something entirely of my own choosing, something that does not capture me but is to be captured by me. The difference between directed and captured attention is the same as the difference between doing things and letting things take their course, or between living and "being lived." No subject could be of greater interest; no subject occupies a more central place in all traditional teachings; and no subject suffers more neglect, misunderstanding, and distortion in the thinking of our modern world.[3]

An inkling of the difficulties encountered in this transition can be gained from Robert Oppenheimer's description of how major scientific breakthroughs occur. He describes a series of "groping, fumbling, tentative efforts" that explore new possibilities and refine old perspectives. The desire to succeed is backed by sustained effort until "error may give way to less error, confusion to less confusion, and bewilderment to insight." Similarly, advancement from any spiral of growth to another is the product of sustained efforts. Except in cases of unusual talent, a person is conscious only of frustrated efforts and flaccid resistance during the initial struggle to outgrow ingrained habits. But with persistence, aspirations become more concrete as resistance is defined, organized, and finally outgrown. The beginning of Spiral IV is therefore a critical period where man must persist in his efforts until he develops the capacity to break free of old habits. If frustration or confusion overwhelm persistence, individual potential will repair to the security of social adult orientation. This retreat is not easy, however, as Thomas Wolff indicated in the title of his classic, *You Can't Go Home Again*. Once one has sensed that life is something more, one's present life is tinctured with a sense of limitation, artificiality or even unreality; a kind of innocence is lost.

Ranging from the demands of environmental necessity to the rigors of monastic life, there are many ways by which social adults can emerge into individuality. But since the specialized way stemming from the functional demands of a society and the existential way developed during the trauma of World War II are widely followed in Western society, these will serve as the foci for analysis.

Complex societies require people who are able to cope with contingencies, solve problems, and guide public taste. Such people do not rely solely upon social norms but are capable of framing and guiding the patterns of a society. For the sake of clarity, those who possess the specialized capacities necessary to organize and direct social response will be called specialized individuals.

Executive administration, scientific research, college teaching, medicine, and military, financial, and political leadership are areas of specialization that direct social adult behavior in reactions to the problems presented by a changing world. On the other side of specialized individuality are the fashion designers, interior decorators, commercial artists, columnists, television directors, and others who profoundly influence public taste. Such positions have their rewards in wealth, power, and prestige within a society. In turn, these rewards, together with the mystiques of leadership, professionalism, sophistication and expertise, serve as lures to draw social adults along well-worn paths to specialized individuality.

More than any other concept, the word *ambition* captures the motivational drive necessary to complete the transition into specialized individuality. But ambition is only part of the general scheme used by societies or subsocieties to encourage the development of specialized individuals. The range of candidates for specialization can be severely limited by the rigid class structure of a theocracy or aristocracy, for example, or almost unlimited in an expanding technological society. Whatever the method for creating a reservoir of potential specialists, those who are candidates are given opportunities to develop an interest in particular endeavors chosen by themselves or their parents, often channeled by school, religious organization and local community, depending on the structure of a society or subsociety. In America the poor can adhere to the path described by Horatio Alger or rise through the hierarchies of labor unions and business organizations, while those from the middle or upper-class backgrounds can enter junior executive programs, train for professions, or undergo concentrated specialization in the graduate programs of the modern university.

During the process of specialized training, the adolescent will normally grow into social adulthood. Within this area of specialization, black-or-white perspectives are gradually refined to accommodate shades of gray, but as suggested in the previous section the remainder of his activities are centered in social orientation. Eventually the promising specialist is encouraged to focus all his energy upon one particular activity. This means plunging beyond social adulthood into a world where ambiguity, risk, and pressure play central roles. It is at this point that the attractive powers of ambition, rewards, and mystique become important, for the social adult is obliged to renounce the security of a socially oriented life in which he now has the skills to live with relative ease. If the evolving adult does take the plunge, he will focus all the sensitivity and social understanding gained from previous experience upon specific capabilities. Then through hard work, frequent decision making, intense competition, and rigorous self-discipline, he will forge the specialized identity that promises both personal and social satisfaction.

Because the transition to individuality develops the capacity to regulate personal action and thought by self-determined criteria, instead of simply internalizing impressions from without, the specialized individual can determine "what's right" within his sphere of interest. This gives him enormous flexibility in how he approaches his subject or other people, for he can innovate to meet each new problem. When this power is mastered, the move to "expert" and management positions is almost assured; and thereafter the ability to handle contingencies is exercised in directing or influencing the lives of others. The difference between the specialized individual who seems to discern correctness in his sphere of interest and the specialized individual who seems dogmatically to assert it—between the knower and the manipulator—is rooted in the integrity cultivated in the social adult stage.

The way through which specialized individuals develop produces several problems requiring brief consideration. The most obvious stem from striving for rewards. Competition for wealth or status in a society can result in self-righteous conflicts such as the contemporary disagreements between medical doctors, osteopaths, and nutritionists. In addition, specialists tend to go where the rewards are, producing effects like the "brain drain" from one country to another. The desire for wealth and prestige can create an abundance of experts in one field and a scarcity in another—as in India where there are many lawyers and few agronomists. But beyond these effects, and much more significant, is the fact that specialized individuality is grounded in one sphere of interest. Social adult norms tend to persist unchallenged outside the sphere. If physicians or generals, for example, become involved in politics, their opinions are often strikingly naive, especially when compared to the extent of their understanding of medicine or warfare. Most experts are aware of their limitations and try to remain within their area of specialization, but occasionally their limitations come crashing through with logical fallacies like "What's good for General Motors is good for America." On the other hand, rarely, the discipline a specialized individual masters in one area is used to bring fresh perspectives to another.

Metaphorically, the specialized individual develops like a man with huge arms that dwarf the rest of his body. Because his future depends exclusively upon the use of those arms, he has limited opportunity to exercise other capacities. Higher status, more power, greater wealth, new fascinations and knowledge continually beckon. Arms may get longer and larger at the expense of other capacities, until strength and cleverness meet their match in competition or exhaustion. And lurking in the background is the prospect of inadequacy in the face of new challenges or the threat of displacement by others more competent than himself. Specialized individuality is socially necessary but leads to personal insecurity and never is quite complete as a spiral of growth.

A sharp contrast exists between these avenues to individuality and the avenue depicted by existential writers. The existential way leads not to specialized individuality but to an undivided, complete individuality. The transformation stems not from the reorganization of perspectives within a society but from profound desire for independence that transcends social orientation. Here the felt inadequacy of social orientation gives rise to dissociation from social norms, values, and sentiments as irrelevant to the basic purpose of life. Dissociation can take the form of monastic retreat, simple withdrawal, or active rejection of society. Whatever the form, it sets the scene for a struggle between social trust and mistrust that eventually leads to thorough self-orientation.

The desire for independence and the humbling question of choice are rooted much deeper in human history than the Homeric legends that inspired ancient Greece. The fundamental significance of this drive has been apprehended in Western thought since the idea of free will emerged in ancient religious and philosophic doctrines. In recent years, existential writers have again formulated a way to self-orientation through personal choice or free will—an "existential way to Individuality" which speaks directly to many problems faced by modern man.

Disillusioned by world wars, economic depression, and the collapse of social idealism, a group of European writers (since called Existentialists) turned from tradition to self-direction to discover meaning in life. In so doing, they reestablished one of the oldest paths to individuality. Although the bitterness of disillusionment is felt in their judgment of social values and outside goals, their substitution of moral responsibility for moral fatalism echoes advice given over the ages to shun society in the pursuit of inner meaning or "authentic existence." Aloneness, despair, and anguish capture the sense of the struggle necessary to emerge as an independent being and sustain the weight of life lived as a constant and imperative choice between "being and nothingness."

The flavor of the "leap into authentic existence" is dramatically described by Camus in *The Stranger*. A social adult, in an aimless search for meaning, becomes involved in both rejecting and embracing the absurdity of life. Plunged into meaninglessness and despair, "the stranger" suddenly transcends chaos to find his authentic self:

> I started yelling at the top of my voice. I hurled insults. . . . It was as if that great rush of anger washed me clean. . . . And I, too, felt ready to start life all over again.[4]

The poetic substance of this transformation is again caught in the final sentence of *The Rebel*:

> The bow bends; the wood complains. At the moment of supreme tension, there will leap into flight an unswerving arrow, a shaft that is inflexible and free.[5]

Camus' description of the final step from mean-
ingfulness to individuality is not simply a flight of poetic
fancy, but the dramatic portrayal of resolution to the
existential crisis. Psychologist Frederick Weiss, for example, has quoted Camus as literary background for the
observation that "total emotional involvement in rage
and conflict often precedes the acceptance of self."[6] Jung
also notes that many of his patients "simply outgrow a
problem which destroyed others":

> This outgrowing, as I formerly called it, on further
> experience was seen to consist in a new level of con-
> sciousness....What on a lower level, had led to the
> wildest conflicts and to panicky outbursts of emo-
> tion, viewed from the higher level of personality,
> now seemed like a storm in the valley seen from a
> high mountain-top.[7]

In terms of the present analysis, Camus, Weiss, and
Jung indicate that behavior resembling neurosis can be
symptomatic of a "normative crisis" that disappears
with the birth of a new spiral of growth.

Camus' "stranger" achieves his creative breakthrough
just before he is to be executed. For Camus, the realization is the product of recognizing the inherent absurdity
of existence and therefore of social values: growth and
choice are rooted in individual awareness. Jean-Paul
Sartre, however, locates choice and growth in authentic
observation, perceiving without the mediation of
cliches and predetermined categories. For Camus, the
authenticity of values remains as moot as the reality of
the individual, while for Sartre they are phe-
nomenologically derived from human nature. It is
not surprising, therefore, that Camus is more attractive
to psychologists of psychoanalytic persuasions, and
Sartre to psychologists involved with philosophical
perspectives. Both sense the absurdity of the conven-

tional world, but Sartre is repeating in modern idiom many of the insights cultivated in Mahayana Buddhism and Zen, and pointed out by Christian mystics as diverse as Nicholas of Cusa and Meister Eckhart.

Flights of arrows and leaps into authenticity are difficult to grasp in any concrete fashion if the underlying process is not thoroughly understood. Perhaps the simplest way of examining what "embracing the absurd" means is to equate it with Descartes' idea of "systematic doubt." Doubting everything that can conceivably be doubted is a formula for breaking up the black-or-white perspectives which dominate the social adult world: rigid values related to success, failure, friends, play, or evil melt before a skeptical onslaught. Transitional dilemmas—vagueness, ambiguity, flux—must be embraced to create a new value structure. But this new value structure is not simply a process of redefinition of what, for instance, "success" means. Rather it is a totally new perspective founded in continual choice. Choice, then, becomes a self-oriented basis for thought and action. In the final leap, one chooses to be authentic.

Proponents of religious doctrines have been deeply concerned with their equivalents of the existential crisis, and for good reason. On one level the question of choice or free will defines man's relationship to God, and the quality of choices made in life determines man's fate after death. When an existential crisis takes place in a religious context, it leads to full assumption of choice through a test of faith that is ultimately a struggle for immortality. To help their members through this struggle, religions provide a framework for self-understanding as well as a refuge where the crisis can take place. Monastic orders, for example, offer orderliness and rigor in everyday life as an anchorage for growth, and guidance by faith in an ultimate order beyond personal confusion as sustenance during the darkest hours before transformation. Ruysbroeck spoke of having to stand nude before the Divine, and John of the Cross spoke of the "dark night of the Soul." Great monastic mystics such as these have insisted that the supports do not vitiate the requirement that one must choose to be authentic.

The role of philosophy parallels that of religion by providing a protective framework for the transition to individuality. Following the secularization of thought in the seventeenth century, the stability of physical order governed by natural law replaced divine order as support for emerging individuality. But as the existence of God was subject to skepticism, so was physical order. Even though Newton's wondrously mechanical universe was later augmented by faith in inevitable progress and purposeful evolution, the stability of physical order melted before relativity and the collapse of social idealism in the twentieth century. As faith in universal order and progress withered, the existential crisis was removed from its protective covering to become a naked struggle with and for oneself, a day-to-day, choice-to-choice contest for existence on the razor's edge between "being and nothingness," between life and death. It is important to note that where Carmus' "stranger" was alone, those who follow existential philosophy at least have a framework for understanding personal chaos. This framework is not a dogmatic creed, however. It is an awareness of the dialectical potentiality between opposites, an awareness that can be generated only from within.

Daniel Levinson's study of the life cycle indicates that if the step to individuality does not occur during early adulthood, many social adults face what he calls "becoming one's own man" around age forty:

> Some men do very little questioning or searching
> during the Mid-Life transition....But for the great
> majority of men—about 80 percent of our sub-
> jects—this period evokes tumultuous struggles within
> the self and with the external world. Their Mid-Life
> Transition is a time of moderate or severe crisis.
> Every aspect of their lives comes into question, and
> they are horrified by much that is revealed. They are
> full of recriminations against themselves and others.
> They cannot go on as before but need time to choose
> a new path or modify the old one.[8]

However, there are large numbers who fail to grow due
to lack of inner and/or outer resources: "It is not at all
certain, of course, that development will occur in middle adulthood. For large numbers of men, life in the
middle years is a process of gradual or rapid stagnation,
or alienation from the world and from the self."[9] The
impulse to mature never dies—it draws one forward to
new horizons or ossifies, but it never just "goes away."

It is not surprising that the mainstream of society does
not easily accommodate the chaos of an existential crisis
or a chaotic "Mid-Life Transition." Systematic doubt
and erratic behavior are generally met with repression.
For this reason those engaged in the transition have
traditionally retreated to "expatriate" life abroad, extended travel, or to the Bohemian fringe at the edge of
society. However, with the secularization of society and
the spread of liberal education—reinforced by interest in
psychology and oriental religions such as Zen—the
existential way has been opened to new varieties of
people, young and old, in all walks of life. As a result,
increasing numbers of people within society are systematically doubting the prevailing norms, values, and sentiments of their society. The whole social-adult

specialized-individual world is under attack from within.

For many young social adults, the existential problem begins to crystallize when they enter college. As many college students are products of middle-class backgrounds, they are usually ambitious and goal oriented toward specialized individuality. However, in the process of acquiring an education they take required courses in comparative religion or philosophy, meet students and professors with values different from their own, and run directly into skepticism and doubt. Provoked or encouraged to explore themselves and their values, they frequently enter a prolonged internal conflict between specialized and existential ways to individuality. Caught between ambition and the lure of independence, ambition is at odds with anguish, and concentration on a particular goal is eroded by uncertainty.

While colleges become tension-filled refuges for the existential crisis, the rest of society has not escaped unscathed. Whenever the solidity of black-or-white perspectives is fractured, doubt and the existential crisis can emerge. While this can happen to anyone, it is those social adults with valuable skills who present the most visible problems for society. Whether shocked by personal or social distress, or repulsed in the climb to specialized individuality, their background rarely prepares them for retreat to the Bohemian fringe or extended travel abroad. Moreover, they generally lack intellectual preparation as a protective framework for growth. Wrought by confusion, their erratic or defiant behavior will meet a variety of negative sanctions such as exclusion from clubs and unions and ridicule by family or friends. They may find themselves opposed by spouses, children, parents, colleagues, employers and the occupational system within which they work—the implicit web of social conformity that seeks to maintain order and prevent unpredictable change. Vested interests and those who maintain the status quo, the groups made famous as the power elite in C. Wright Mills' work, often go to considerable lengths to keep employees in line. Describing this trend, sociologist Peter Berger writes:

> Enlightened bureaucratic management...no longer throws its deviant employees out on the street, but instead compels them to undergo treatment by its consulting psychiatrists. In this way, the deviant individual (that is, the one who does not meet the criteria of normality set up by the management, or by the bishop) is still threatened with unemployment and with the loss of social ties, but in addition he is also stigmatized as one who might very well fall outside the pale of responsible men altogether, unless he can give evidence of remorse ("insight") and resignation ("response to treatment"). Thus the innumerable "counseling," "guidance," and "therapy" programs developed in many sectors of contemporary social life greatly strengthen the control apparatus of the society as a whole and especially those parts of it where the sanctions of the politico-legal system cannot be invoked.[10]

Whether in college or not, those caught between ambition and the desire for independence can experience a long and chaotic struggle that produces profoundly disturbed personalities until the transition ends in individuality or exhaustion. However, disturbance in any spiral does not automatically lead to imprisonment in that spiral or distortion in a higher spiral. It may reflect the inchoate need to progress to a new level. In some

Polynesian societies, for example, what might readily be diagnosed as schizophrenia is seen as a crisis of individuality fraught with dangers but full of promise. The individual may suffer further personality disintegration, or he may emerge triumphant on a new level of awareness, complete with new prestige and social recognition.

Commenting on the increasing confusion inherent in this transition, Erikson points to "matters of identity" as the "major problem" faced by psychologists:

> To condense it into a formula: the patient of today suffers most under the problem of what he should believe in and who he should—or, indeed, might—be or become, while the patient of early psychoanalysis suffered most under inhibitions which prevented him from being what and who he thought he knew he was....And so it comes about that we begin to conceptualize matters of identity at the very time in history when they become a problem.[11]

Erikson has hit upon a tremendous insight here. In the very areas where a society begins to fail to minister to the needs of its members, self-conscious analysis arises. Mircea Eliade has pointed to the rise of the social sciences, especially psychology, sociology and anthropology, during the last century and a half as evidence of the loss of social cycles, rites of passage, normative agreement, and participatory rituals. We gain awareness because we have *lost* something. As described by Jung, "the unconscious becomes conscious."

This transitional analysis has concentrated upon the specialized and existential ways to individuality because they are the most prominent in modern Western society. However, there are other ways that should at least be mentioned. Several religious sects instill a basis for individuality. The Quaker, for example, is taught to listen to a small but commanding voice from within that guides him, toward an "inner light." By teaching a person to cultivate inner direction, such doctrines provide a sound basis for transition to individuality. Along these same lines, any form of sustained meditation under guidance by a master will accomplish similar results by directing attention away from the social adult center of orientation. Many teachers of meditation insist that different forms of meditation lead to different goals—an indication that inner states are as diverse as external phenomena—but all agree that the beginning of meditation is a significant turning within.

Another way into individuality is the response called forth by an acute social crisis or revolution. When social values begin to crash on all sides, the opportunities and needs for individuals become acute, and many will rise to meet the occasion. Conflicts between individuals created under such circumstances blister the period during and after social upheavals. Given the social ferment throughout most of the modern world, the revolutionary way to individuality warrants careful study.

Whatever the path of mid-life transition, the odyssey to individuality is not easy. When a social adult first attempts to evoke more evolved consciousness, he is plagued by doubts and frustration. But as old patterns are unlearned or renounced, he begins to add something of his own to impressions internalized from outside. As he begins to regulate his behavior and objectives through conclusions arrived at from within, he begins to determine his own way through life instead of drifting with the current of outside circumstances. Eventually he finds a sense of pleasure and satisfaction in his personal uniqueness and initiative. As Levinson states in his study of the adult life-cycle:

If he is to make significant mid-life changes in love
relationships, occupation, leisure and other important aspects of his life, a man must become more
individuated. He must confront the great polarities
that are the basic divisions in the individual and in
society. In successive developmental periods from infancy through old age, especially the major transitions, a man has an opportunity to reduce the internal splitting. Though he can never entirely overcome
the divisions, he finds new ways of being
Young/Old, Masculine/Feminine, Destruc-
tive/Creative and Attached/Separate, according to
his place in the life cycle.[12]

It is only through constant striving that men and
women can develop more comprehensive vistas for life.
Whether motivated by ambition or a desire for independence, the budding individual should nourish and
strengthen the goals that appeal to this mind. Through
persistent efforts and personal goals, he will evoke
capabilities that would otherwise never unfold. Man
may be born like a prince destined to wear a crown, but
he must first develop the capacities necessary to rule his
own realm.

Spiral IV

The Individual

In Spiral IV the fires of uniqueness lying deep within blaze forth in self-assertion to provide the basis for leading, changing, and challenging the world of social adults. In contrast to the usual idea that all men are unique and therefore "individual," Spiral IV will be called the individual spiral of growth because the self has asserted its uniqueness to become the center of orientation. Where the social adult acts according to programs provided by his society or subculture, the individual programs himself.

The distinctive characteristics of life beyond the realm of social adulthood have received extensive consideration in poetry, drama, literature, philosophy and theology. During the last hundred years the subject has been systematically explored through ideas such as Kierkegaard's "authentic existence," Heidegger's "self-manifestation," Freud's "total personality," George Herbert Mead's "I," Abraham Maslow's "self-actualization," and Jung's idea of "Individuation." While each of these approaches describes an evolved self as a focus for personal action and thought, each tends to place the upper ranges of human consciousness within one large and complex category.

The qualitative difference between Spirals III and IV was concisely described by George Herbert Mead in *Mind, Self and Society,* published in 1934. In this classic sociological treatise, Mead presented behavior in society as dependent upon a "me" that resembles social adulthood, or an "I" that approximates individuality. The "me" is dominated by the values, norms, and sentiments of society while "I" stands for the ability to influence the process of social adaptation and growth. The I grows from me as a person develops the capacity to put himself in the place of others, and thereby has access to more than one me as a source of reference and innovation. A unique I unfolds as if a socially oriented person would examine himself to say, "Here are the social values, norms and sentiments; here is me; what can I do with this structure and myself?" The I reveals itself through "initiative, novelty, and uniqueness" to find gratifying experience where social situations permit self-expression. In this process the me expands to become a firm basis for creative behavior in society. Paradoxically, individuation depends upon the ability to put oneself in the place of another.

With the qualitative distinction between social adulthood and individuality established, the web of complexity behind "initiative, novelty, and uniqueness" can be untangled by making a distinction between esthetics and logic, as contrasted with emotions and intellect. As previously described, Spiral III behavior and thought are rooted in a tension between the emotions and the intellect. When individuality emerges, the emotions and the intellect are dialectically transformed into the more evolved capacities of esthetics and logic.

Esthetics as used in this analysis is a synthesis between the emotions and the intellect where the emotions have been refined and purposefully channeled from within; or simply put, esthetics is a refinement of *emotion with systematic governance.* Logic takes the intellect beyond Piaget's "phase of formal operations," through a synthesis between the intellect and the emotions, where rational activity is emotionally charged for more effective thought. Logic is, in short, a refinement of *reason with regulated emotional content.* Whatever the path taken to Spiral IV, esthetics and logic are the source of the individual's "initiative, novelty, and uniqueness." They are, therefore, the keys to understanding the self-assertive complexities in Spiral IV.

Although esthetics and logic are characterized in terms rather different from ordinary usage, this departure is not arbitrary. Immanuel Kant's lectures in anthropology, for instance, describe "a science of sensuousness, namely esthetics, and a science of understanding, namely logic." Abraham Maslow made a subtler distinction when he examined self-actualized people, "finding in them simultaneously the ability to abstract without giving up concreteness and the ability to be concrete without giving up abstractness." These abilities precisely delineate logical and esthetic capacities. The "ability to abstract without giving up concreteness" would, for example, characterize the physical scientist who is theoretically imaginative without abandoning empirical research, while "the ability to be concrete without giving up abstractness" portrays the artist who organizes his compositions without abandoning the esthetic creativity of his work.

Whether applied to esthetic or logical individuals, Maslow's description discloses another characteristic of Spiral IV; the free flow between abstract and concrete, as distinguished from the social adult dichotomy between abstract and concrete. As Maslow indicates, the interrelationship between abstract and concrete allows confident and harmonious action in situations where the social adult would be confused and frustrated. Both esthetic and logical capacities provide a basis for effective observation, discrimination, and concentration. This study will take esthetic and logical individuals as types which are exemplified in various degrees in all people. The aim is not to categorize men and women dogmatically but to understand the dynamics of growth.

Although logical or esthetic capabilities give the individual considerable effectiveness, they also set parameters. When the logical individual encounters a problem that logic cannot resolve, he will respond with social adult emotion; and when the esthetic individual cannot resolve a problem with esthetics, he must resort to social adult reason. It is also apparent that individuals with logical capacity do their best work after the long struggle for self-orientation has brought the emotions under control.

While the logical individual works best under stable circumstances, this is frequently not the case with the esthetic individual. Esthetic capabilities are generated during transition when intense emotional interaction gives rise to insights that can be incorporated into successful work. Thus the transition to individuality can be a productive period that paves the way for serious trouble when the stability of Spiral IV arrives. If an artist, for example, has become dependent upon the hyperstimulation that accompanies transition, he will find himself severed from his source of emotional stimulation when he becomes a mature esthetic individual. It is therefore not uncommon for an author or poet to produce one or two good books during a period of internal turmoil, only to dissolve into mediocrity when stability arrives. It is just as common for the individual writer or painter to turn to the stimulation of alcohol, drugs or a life of desperate abandon in an attempt to perpetuate or recreate emotional excitement. Malcolm Lowry, for example, apparently wrote *Under the Volcano*, his great work, during the transition to individuality but found himself unable to produce another volcano within the relative calm of individuality. Desperately seeking renewal in the artificial stimulation of alcohol, he soon destroyed himself. Dylan Thomas went through a similar phase of creativity to become what he felt was a "has-been," and he too fled into alcoholism.

The lives of Lowry, Thomas, and countless others have ended in early death or mediocrity because they could not reconcile stability with the transitional dynamics they relied upon as successful artists. Yet such tragedy is unnecessary because individuality actually liberates new and more powerful sensibilities. When esthetic individuals abandon hyperemotional stimulation and begin to explore their new sensitivities, they can uncover reservoirs of creative potential deep within themselves. These can be as profound as those reflected in the works of Rembrandt, Velásquez, Titian, Cézanne, T. S. Eliot, and the other great artists throughout culture history. Psychologists with experience in psychoanalytic practice have come to suspect the Freudian view that esthetic creativity arises out of profound psychic tensions. Karen Horney and Rollo May, for example, flatly reject such propositions. May holds that creativity is bound up with a mature release of the capacity to love, and Horney argued that the artist is creative in spite of inner tensions.

As previously suggested, in some individuals esthetic and logical capacities are balanced. This equilibrium can be achieved in two ways. First, the emotion and intellect can develop simultaneously into esthetic sensibility and logical precision. Individuals who develop in this way tend to rise from environments where cultural roots are deep and the pressure to specialize is minimal, where family life is full and stable, where broad education is readily available, and where personal crises are accepted and quitely assimilated into the family and community. Although pockets of balanced stability have never been abundant, the Jeffersons and Voltaires who embodied the balance of their early environments have left remarkable contributions.

The second way to balanced individuality begins when an esthetic or logical individual puts aside his main source of strength to systematically develop its counterpart capacity. There are many reasons why an individual might undertake this effort. He might be motivated by an internal compulsion, inspired by others, bored with specialized success, fascinated by other realms of endeavor, or simply drawn by the desire to expand personal horizons. But sustained effort, sometimes accompanied by bewilderment and even resistance from family and friends, is always necessary.

In spite of the difficulty in attaining both esthetic and logical capacities, balanced individuality is highly desirable. On one side, there is little possibility of a balanced individual regressing to social adult emotion or intellect when threatened by a personal crisis. On the other hand, the two capacities together provide greater scope for the resolution of the problem. When the self is the center of orientation, the ego demands both exercise and protection, and interacting esthetic and logical capacities are powerful resources for defense as well as assertion.

Even light casts its shadow. While Spiral IV has its normal or healthy dimensions in esthetic, logical or balanced individuals, there is also an abnormal or pathological side. Just as the structure of Spiral III can produce an infantile-adult, Spiral IV discloses a childish-individual. Whether the impetus comes from parental pressures or sheer genius, a talented child can use adolescence to prepare for specialized individuality at the expense of social-adult orientation. The result is the childish individual who fails to develop sensitivity toward others or an awareness of "what's right" in his society. Such a person therefore, does not incorporate the solidity of the social-adult world into his center of individual orientation. In exaggerated forms the childish individual has been portrayed through folk, literary, and electronic media as the antihero: the capable but "mad" scientist, the "egghead" intellectual, the ruthless businessman, the exotic woman who is diabolically calculating in the manipulation of men because her beauty and intelligence have encouraged treatment as an individual since childhood. Beyond such examples, all childish individuals share the tendency to use others as simple objects to manipulate and control. Others are items in a world of objects to be treated as means to the childish individual's ends, and never as ends in themselves.

The possibility of the childish individual assuming the extreme forms described above would depend upon the completeness of the infant and child orientations, the degree of social adulthood assimilated, and the circumstances in which he finds himself as an individual. With self-orientation founded on a tenuous basis, it is common for such a person to seek extremely stable environments dominated by powerful mother or father figures who rigidly maintain the "decisiveness of relationships" characteristic of the family. The "mad" scientist sheltered in a corporation laboratory or the woman dominated by a very strong husband can lead quite positive lives. When stable circumstances collapse or are not established, trouble usually erupts. Stability, for instance, can center wholly within the self to produce the familiar egomaniac, or it can center on an idea to produce a Messianic fanatic. Many of the problems presented by childish individuals stem from their tendency to revert to childhood patterns of behavior when beset by personal crises, behavior that can assume diabolic proportion when it is supported by brilliant esthetic or logical capacities. It is precisely because the childish individual brings highly developed capacities to immature goals that this condition is called "childish" and not "childlike." There is nothing innocent in this behavior, though much of it may be unconscious.

Aside from childish individuals, much of human history can be understood as a struggle to attain and contain individuality. While the Greek and Roman worlds cultivated individuality, they well understood that self-orientation was a mixed blessing, that it brought power in society as well as self-direction, that venal opportunism was as likely a product as enlightened leadership. Socrates' complaints against the sophists, as preserved in the dialogues of Plato, can be seen as criticism of the kind of individuality fostered by sophistic modes of education with their promise of crude social success. In spite of this awareness, by the time of Alcibiades and the Peloponnesian Wars Athens was undermined by rampant individuality, and Rome suffered a similar fate with the disintegration of the Republic. The medieval Church, surrounded by a rampaging feudal nobility, frantically strove to curb individual ambition and pride with doctrines of moderation, humility, and charity. Nothing was more antipathetic to the medieval Christian ideal than pride, "the whole puddle and sink of all sins against God and man." Yet even the medieval Church, already corrupted from within, succumbed when its status, wealth, and privilege became a prize for the self-seeking ambition of the Borgia and Medici families.

During the fifteenth and sixteenth centuries the cult of the individual swept Western Europe. Where the medieval Church had thundered against pride, the savants of fifteenth century Italy urged pride in accomplishment and exalted personal uniqueness, while Protestant reformers hailed religion as a personal relationship between each man and God. In both the north and the south, men were judged by talent, wealth and accomplishment, and individualism was soon enthroned throughout Western society.

But with the new framework of self-exaltation, attempts were made to restrain capricious opportunism. In southern Europe the ideal of the "universal man" who cultivates all aspects of life helped to balance opportunism, while northern Protestantism developed doctrines of social responsibility. With entrepreneurial capitalism—perhaps the supreme focus for self-assertion—doctrines of "stewardship of wealth" or philanthropy were urged from pulpit and podium in attempts to restrain self-seeking ambition.

This historical resume does not discount the many individual accomplishments and contributions in all realms of human endeavor, but it acknowledges limitations that pervade the modern world. Due to endless possibilities for specialization, as well as circumstances conducive to existential transformation, the modern world represents an apotheosis of the Apollonian ideal in the form of rational self-assertion. But the very degree of success presents civilization with grave problems.

The patterns of disintegration set by Greece, Rome, and the medieval Church can be avoided today only if modern civilization succeeds in eliminating the bottle-neck created by the enthronement of individuality. Esthetic and logical powers rooted in self-orientation are simply too limited for the scope of our increasingly complex and interdependent world. Individual limitations have become a straight-jacket for human expression and creative concern in both society and personal lives.

Individual—Free Person Transition

Beyond Spiral IV lie awesome possibilities that beckon most individuals at some point in their lives. The urge to transcend self-orientation is often stifled by a resilient and successful ego. Yet the call echoes throughout history:

> Whosoever shall seek to save his life
>   shall lose it;
> And whosoever shall lose his life shall
>   preserve it.
>
> Jesus

> He who humbles himself shall be saved;
> He who bends shall be made straight;
> He who empties himself shall be filled.
>
> Lao Tzu

> A death blow is a life blow to some
> Who, till they died, did not alive become;
> Who, had they lived, had died, but when
> They died, vitality begun.
>
> Emily Dickinson

Quick now, here, now, always—
A condition of complete simplicity
(Costing no less than everything)
And all shall be well and
All manner of things shall be well.

T. S. Eliot

Die and become.
Till thou has learned this
Thou art but a dull guest
On this dark planet.

Goethe

Die to the lesser and become the greater—a touch-stone for the enrichment of human life, yet difficult to grasp. As Gail Sheehy states in *Passages*:

> The mystics and the poets always get there first. Shakespeare tried to tell us that man lives through seven stages in the "All the world's a stage" speech in *As You Like It*. And many centuries before Shakespeare, the Hindu scriptures in India described four distinct states, each calling for its own fresh response: student; householder; retirement, when the individual was encouraged to become a pilgrim and begin his true education as an adult; and the final state of *sannyasin*, defined as "one who neither hates nor loves anything."[1]

While the idea of a second birth has been described by poets and mystics and has been included in every great religion and philosophy to inspire many men and women, it has not been carefully considered among the doctrines that motivate our modern world. However, from Eric Erikson to Abraham Maslow and Lawrence Kohlberg, a new trend is emerging. Lawrence Kohlberg's philosophy of moral development has evolved

beyond his earlier work to propose a "Stage 7" level
that would seem to correspond with the next spiral of
growth. Kohlberg's "Stage 7" goes beyond Erikson's
theory of a final step in the life cycle where integrity is
juxtaposed with despair. Kohlberg notes that the
possibility of despair is not automatically mitigated by
awareness of universal principles. Such awareness may
lead to despairing of ever finding justice in the world.
Even after one has overcome questions of moral principle, one can still ask why one should be moral at all.
Seriously pursued questions of value invariably lead to
more fundamental philosophical problems, and so the
question "Why be moral?" can lead to the questions
"Why live?" and "How is one to face death?" The out-
worn categories familiar to dichotomous thinking are
useless here. Contemplation is required, a new intimacy
with the reality of one's experience, sometimes but not
necessarily expressed in terms of union with the Divine,
yet always involving a universal perspective, a connec-
tion with something beyond the self:

> In the state of mind we have metaphorically termed
> Stage 7 we identify ourselves with the cosmic or
> infinite perspective itself; we value life from its
> standpoint. At such a time, what is ordinarily back-
> ground becomes foreground and the self is no longer
> figure to the ground. We sense the unity of the whole
> and ourselves as part of that unity.[2]

Until modern psychology follows the lead provided
by men like Kohlberg and Maslow, we will not have
a clear picture of this transformation in human consciousness. Even when ancient doctrines speak clearly,
they no longer capture the imagination of most people in
the West. Mahayana Buddhism's *Lankavatara Sutra*,
for example, is specific in describing "die and become"

as "the turning about in the deepest seat of consciousness...where compassion for others transcends all thoughts of self."[3] Yet when measured by empirical standards this statement is hardly more concrete than the idea of a second birth.

In the absence of more specific psychological data, the best approach to the problem of a second birth is through the testimony of eminent individuals who have asked the ultimate questions, confronted despair, and experienced "the turning about in the deepest seat of consciousness."

Tolstoy left a particularly poignant description of the esthetic individual transition to a deeper and more comprehensive spiral of consciousness. In examining this confession it should be remembered that Tolstoy had no guidelines for growth and was obliged to struggle with the clinging core of his individuality in total darkness:

> I felt that something had broken within me on which my life had always rested, that I had nothing left to hold onto, and that morally my life had stopped. An invisible force impelled me to get rid of my existence, in one way or another. It cannot be said exactly that I *wished* to kill myself, for the force which drew me away from life was fuller, more powerful, more general than any mere desire. It was a force like my old aspiration to live, only it impelled me in the opposite direction. It was an aspiration of my whole being to get out of life.
>
> Behold me then, a man happy and in good health, hiding the rope in order not to hang myself to the rafters of the room where every night I went to sleep alone; behold me no longer going shooting, lest I should yield to the too easy temptation of putting an end to myself with my gun.
>
> I did not know what I wanted. I was afraid of life; I was driven to leave it; and in spite of that I still hoped something from it.

All this took place at a time when so far as my outer circumstances went, I ought to have been completely happy. I had a good wife who loved me and whom I loved; good children and a large property which was increasing with no pains taken on my part. I was more respected by my kinsfolk and acquaintances than I had ever been; I was loaded with praise by strangers; and without exaggeration I could believe my name already famous. Moreover I was neither insane nor ill. On the contrary, I possessed a physical and mental strength which I have rarely met in persons of my age. I could mow as well as the peasants, I could work with my brain eight hours uninterrupted and feel no bad effects.

And yet I could give no reasonable meaning to my life. And I was surprised that I had not understood this from the very beginning. My state of mind was as if some wicked and stupid jest was being played upon me by someone. One can live only so long as one is intoxicated, drunk with life; but when one grows sober one cannot fail to see that it is all a stupid cheat. What is truest about it is that there is nothing even funny or silly in it; it is cruel and stupid, purely and simply. . . .

This is no fable, but the literal incontestable truth which everyone may understand. What shall be the outcome of what I do today? Of what I shall do tomorrow? What will be the outcome of all my life? Why should I live? Why should I do anything? Is there in life any purpose which the inevitable death which awaits me does not undo and destroy?

These questions are the simplest in the world. From the stupid child to the wisest old man, they are in the soul of every human being. Without an answer to them, it is impossible, as I experienced, for life to go on.

The source of Tolstoy's future strength was uncovered when persistent probing gradually revealed a more evolved perspective in which old problems were resolved:

> I began to see that I had no right to rely on my individual reasoning and neglect these answers given by faith...I was saved from suicide. Just how or when the change took place I cannot tell. But as insensibly and gradually as the force of life had been annulled within me, and I had reached my moral death-bed, just as gradually and imperceptibly did the energy of life come back....I gave up the life of the conventional world, recognizing it to be no life, but a parody on life, which its superfluities simply keep us from comprehending....[4]

With the "turning about" completed, Tolstoy's remaining years were devoted to a life "where compassion for others transcends all thoughts of self."

While Tolstoy's blind struggle illustrates the process of self-inquiry through which esthetic individuals "die and become," the recorded picture of the logical individual transformation is markedly different. Where the esthetic individual will develop by following his sensibilities through evolving turmoil to the next spiral of growth, the transformation of a logical individual is frequently so sudden that it is accompanied by an "illumination" or "enlightment" experience. Such illuminations can be simply defined as implosions of sudden insight that fuse a deeper or more comprehensive level of consciousness.

An ecstatic description of sudden enlightenment was recorded by the remarkable seventeenth-century philosopher-scientist Blaise Pascal. Eight years before this experience Pascal embraced the primacy of religious revelation but continued to give first consideration to his scientific work. Contradictions between religious belief and scientific effort steadily intensified until a "fiery vision" fused a new foundation for his life. Pascal's "Memorial," a spontaneous record of that vision, is now one of the treasures of the Bibliothèque nationale in Paris:

> From about half past ten in the evening until half past twelve, FIRE. Certitude, certitude, feeling, joy, peace....Joy, joy, joy, tears of joy...Jesus Christ. I have been separated from him; I have fled from him, renounced him, crucified him. Let me never be separated from him....Renunciation, total and sweet.

After the vision Pascal's efforts were devoted to the idea that men must be concerned with more than daily pleasure or intellectual attainment; and it is due to his later work that he is remembered by all but historians of science.

In 1955 the Jesuit scientist Teilhard de Chardin reflected back to the "revelation" that inspired his lifework:

> It would seem that a single ray of such a light falling at random on the noosphere (mental properties activating evolution) like a spark, must have produced an explosion powerful enough to re-fuse and re-cast the whole face of the world in one instant.
>
> How is it then, that as I look around me, still dazzled by this revelation, I find that I am almost the only one of my species, the only one to have seen it?...And so it is that, when I am asked, I cannot quote a single writer, a single book in which one can find a clear expression of the "diaphany" that has transmuted all things for me....
>
> Evidence, first, of the coherence that this ineffable Element...introduces into the depths of my thought and of my heart.
>
> Evidence, too, of the contagious power of a form of Charity in which it becomes possible to love God

not only "with all one's heart, and all one's soul" but with the universe-in-evolution. . . .

Evidence, finally, of the *superiority* (and at the same time of the *identity*) of what I see, in relation to what I had been taught.[5]

It was this experience that provided the organizing principle behind Teilhard's efforts to blend religion and science. His report illustrates one common though not universal characteristic of such experiences. He sees his experience as wholly new, unique, and heretofore untold, yet even within the Catholic tradition there is a rich literature of just such intense breakthroughs. Surely Teilhard knew of St. John of the Cross, for example, or of Jan van Ruysbroeck, much less St. Paul. The feeling of total freshness—as if the world were just then created in a "Let there be Light"—is not objective datum. Indeed, if this were true the basic proposition of this essay would be destroyed. Nevertheless, it does indicate that the experience is fundamental, deeper, more intense and profound than anything previously witnessed by the subject. Given this, one can forgive an initial presumption to uniqueness, just as, in one's joy that the child has in fact performed the marvel of taking a step, one overlooks the child's feeling that *he alone* has walked for the first time.

A religious enlightenment also transformed the life of an obscure Wall Street broker who is remembered by thousands of recovered alcoholics as Bill:

He was sitting one evening at a kitchen table with a friend he knew as a life-long fellow-alcoholic. He offered this man a drink and was turned down. He was startled. His friend explained that he had joined a religious group which had taught him to believe in God, and he had thereby found the will-power to resist liquor. He (Bill) was dumbfounded. For a

month he continued to drink and to meditate upon
this startling phenomenon. Then he went to a
hospital to...have the whiskey sweated out of him.
Finally, his head was clear. But his spirits were low.
He decided to try to do what his friend had done. He
concentrated on this thought "If there be a God, let
Him show Himself."

The result was instantaneous and incredible. There
was a blinding electric flash of white light. He seemed
to be on a high mountain with a great wind of electric
force blowing through him. His body trembled with
a consuming ecstasy, and a voice spoke these words,
"You are a free man." The ecstasy subsided and he
felt a great peace.[6]

A few months later Bill and a doctor friend founded
Alcoholics Anonymous.

Pascal's "Memorial," Teilhard's "revelation," and
Bill's "white light" are examples of ecstatic transformations with emphatic religious overtones similar to the
well-known visions of St. Paul on the road to Damascus
and St. Augustine in the garden. But such visions can be
predominantly secular as, for example, when Thomas
Hobbes picked up a copy of Euclid in the Cavendish
library, or when Descartes suddenly perceived that the
world was understandable in mathematical terms. The
eighteenth century philosopher Jean-Jacques Rousseau
has also recorded a nonreligious vision on the road to
Vincennes:

> Suddenly I felt my mind dazzled by a thousand
> lights; crowds of lively ideas presented themselves at
> once, with a force and confusion that threw me into
> an inexpressible trouble; I felt my head seized with a
> vertigo like that of intoxication. A violent palpitation
> oppressed me, made me gasp for breath, and being
> unable any longer to breathe as I walked, I let myself
> drop under one of the trees of the wayside, and there
> I spent half an hour in such a state of agitation that

> when I got up I perceived the whole front of my vest
> moistened with my own tears which I had shed
> unawares.[7]

Arthur Koestler, a modern writer and social critic
whose background was not religious, has recorded an
internal transformation without theological overtones.
Koestler's experience occurred while he was a prisoner
in Fascist Spain:

> I was, of course, in prison and might be shot. But this
> was immediately succeeded by...floating on my
> back in a river of peace, under bridges of
> silence....The I had ceased to exist. "Mystical"
> experiences, as we dubiously call them, are not so
> nebulous, vague, or maudlin—they only become so
> when we debase them by verbalization....When I
> say "the I had ceased to exist," I refer to a concrete
> experience that is verbally as incommunicable as the
> feeling aroused by a piano concerto, yet just as
> real....For the first time, the veil has fallen and one
> is in touch with "real reality," the hidden order of
> things....It struck me as self-evident that...we
> were all responsible for each other—not only in the
> superficial sense of social responsibility but because,
> in some inexplicable manner, we partook of the
> same substance of identity, like Siamese twins or
> communicating vessels.[8]

The power of this experience converted Koestler from
communist ideology to the search for more universal
answers to human problems.

These examples not only help to clarify what is meant
by the turning about in the deepest seat of consciousness; they throw considerable light on two
qualities involved in the transformation: personal
experience and the esthetic or logical inclination of
individuality.

The impact of personal experience is evident in each

of the previous examples. While the transformations of St. Paul, Pascal, Bill, and Teilhard were anchored in religious perspectives, the others were grounded in secular world views. Both Descartes and Hobbes were absorbed by the seventeenth century interest in mathematics, and Rousseau's mental fusion built upon the eighteenth century concern with institutional reform. Koestler's sudden perception became the foundation for a new interaction with secular life. It is clear, therefore, that growth beyond individuality is rooted in individual experience within a culture. It is also evident that the transformation results in a deeper and more comprehensive engagement with specific aspects of a culture. All of these men, with the formidable exception of Pascal, were not luminaries of their epochs before their enlightenment experiences. Only after these perceptions did they become influential within their societies.

The above examples also indicate that the transformation is influenced by the esthetic or logical bias of each individual. Esthetic individuals apparently evolve through a process of accumulative turmoil, while logical individuals push self-exploration to explosive limits. In both cases growth is dependent upon tracing out the threads of inner dissonance that isolate and destroy self-orientation.

While all transitions involve a struggle with doubt and frustration, the transition to Spiral V is more uncertain than those that came before because it requires sustained self-conscious effort. Any transition is plagued by reversions to the previous center of orientation, just as the growing infant will cling to his mother's skirts; but for the evolving individual reversion centers on the structure of judgments created in establishing individuality. The result is a ferocious internal struggle where self-inquiry and the desire to grow clash with the ingrained structure of judgments. As the quotation from Tolstoy indicates, old habits can be so tenacious that the evolving individual may be driven to "kill," figuratively or literally, the clinging self. Certainly the individual requires all his powers of self-inquiry, patience, and honesty before the roots of I and not-I can be juxtaposed in creative opposition. These qualities of character, useful at every stage (for they can be observed in rudimentary form even in the child), become critical because assessment of self and social interaction are based on knowledge. In this transition, it becomes clear that the requisite knowledge is increasing self-knowledge and not so-called objective knowledge of the world (the knowledge of the specialized individual). The data for cultivating this knowledge cannot be obtained through dishonesty and techniques of avoidance.

The importance of the internal dialectic of creative oppositions is underscored by sources as diverse as El-Ghazali on Sufism, St. John of the Cross on Christian monasticism, Suzuki on Zen Buddhism, Hegelian philosophy, and Erikson's psychology. John's "to be what you are not, experience what you are not," Buddha's "Middle Way" that persists after every possible negation, the Hegelian idea of dialectic growth, Erikson's counterparts from "basic trust vs. mistrust" to "ego integrity vs. despair,"[9] and Kohlberg's seven stages of moral development—all these signal the human capacity to dissolve restrictions by isolating inner contradictions. Each statement indicates that the individual evolves through persistent self-inquiry until the roots of I and not-I are isolated in creative opposition. The mental fusion described in the previous examples will then reorient the individual's perspective; and the precipitating dilemma will seem like a "storm in the valley seen from a high mountain top." While the enlightenment experience can be neither forced nor guaranteed, all these teachings and theories seem to agree that it is more likely to occur after preparation. Even Bill was first dumbfounded by a previously unconsidered possibility and brooded on it for a time before he conceived the thought which triggered the "explosion." Others could think that thought without any consequences whatsoever.

Where the esthetic or logical individual is prone to dramatic transformation easy to observe, the individual with balanced capacities tends to grow in a subtle and unspectacular manner more difficult to follow. Because balanced capabilities allow great flexibility in the interplay between an individual and his environment, the outgrowing of limitations is accomplished with relative ease. If either esthetic or logical capacities are not withered through excessive preoccupation, continual dialectic interaction will pave the way to Spiral V through gradual refinement of both capacities. What is required is nothing superhuman, but rather the reduction of self-centered activity through the pursuit of universal values. This is accomplished by a cool recognition of the enormous difference between delusive posturing and the real world in which diverse human beings are born, grow old and die, burdened by sorrows caused by their own ignorance. This does not imply the need to commit oneself to some creed or doctrine, for it requires a transcendence of mechanistic, fearful or unthinking adherence. It is a rejection of the preoccupation with self-image and a concern to lay bare the architectonic of the self.

Although balanced individuals have the potential to evolve with seeming ease, few individuals of any type actually make the step to Spiral V. Maslow estimates that only one or two people out of every two hundred are "self-actualizers"—a category that includes all mature individuals as well as more evolved spirals. The struggle for existence is so intense in our affluent society that, as in Alice's *Looking-Glass Land*, it takes all the running we can muster to stay in the same place. Nevertheless, most individuals should be able to continue growing either by developing balanced capabilities or by pushing esthetics or logic to their creative limits. Apparently many individuals fail to evolve because their potentials are not awakened by a sustained awareness or the growth process leading to Spiral V, or because they lack the courage necessary for extensive self-exploration. Many human beings are burdened by an acute sense of mortality, a fear of annihilation or a fear of being nothing, a fear of loss of identity, a perpetual proneness to breakdown and disintegration. One can only wonder how many individuals have been stifled by fear or ignorance, by power and wealth. How many Tolstoys have not been careful to hide their ropes, and how many Pascals have retreated in fear before the onslaught of an enlightenment experience? How many individuals have been overwhelmed by a sense of meaninglessness or a feeling of pervasive futility? Such waste of human potential is a tragedy by any standards, and it indicates a major task for the future: to examine and encourage the process of growth beyond individuality. This transition is difficult because it constitutes the threshold where social conditioning ceases to guide and to coerce the individual. Thus the community cannot help the individual through the transition and, fearing loss of control, he may actually resist rather than let go.

As previously mentioned, scholars like Abraham Maslow are developing a psychology of growth beyond social adulthood. But there are other sources supporting the transition from individuality that should not be dismissed. The various disciplines of Zen Buddhism, for example, have refined methods to provoke transition by forcing the mind into an impasse that results in a sudden leap to *satori* or enlightenment. Rigorous analysis of such methods may yield helpful information. The current widespread interest in meditation and the transpersonal psychology movement are contributing to a growing body of knowledge on reaching higher stages.

It is clear that self-actualization requires something more than preoccupation with interests, fear of loss, and the constant identification of advantages. It involves self-transcendence through seeing beyond oneself to accept the fact that one is not the only person on earth, that the universe is not entirely for one's personal convenience, that the world can be a fascinating place, and that there is nothing threatening about self-forgetfulness. Self-actualization involves a continual expansion of awareness. The more we transcend individuality, the more we self-actualize.

Beyond an understanding of the process leading to transformation, there is a great need for personal guidance and support. It is unfortunate that the individual in transition cannot turn with confidence to psychologists. This is largely because psychological theory is devoted to helping people function as successful social adults and individuals.

Western psychological "help" will often stifle the process of transition by asserting the claims of social orientation on the ego. Despite attempts to bridge the gulf between so-called Eastern and Western psychologies (i.e., D. T. Suzuki's and Erich Fromm's contributions to *Zen Buddhism and Psychoanalysis*), the two are incompatible. The gap is not between East and West, but rather between psychologies of coping and adjustment and psychologies of self-transformation. The first seeks to debug the personality; the second to eradicate it as the active agent of the self. Precisely because a few theorists like Maslow have tried to bridge this gulf, their work is attractive to the general public and intriguing to some professionals, but also violently rejected by others. Nothing less than one's conception of the nature of the human being is at stake in these different approaches.

The idea of the guru or master, although it has been abused and misunderstood in the West, might well be incorporated into psychological theory and practice. The guru does not arbitrarily dictate behavior. Rather he is a person who has grown beyond individuality and studied the process of human growth. The guru is therefore in a position to help the evolving individual maintain opposition and integrity when personal relationships undergo drastic change.

Despite the difficulties encountered in transition, there is good reason to assume that Spiral V lies within the aspiration or reach of most individuals. Although the transition is more profound and complex than those that went before, it is no more mysterious. Just as the flower must die to become fruit, "to die and become" is a step in the normal process of growth in which the individual awakens the perspective of underlying unity among men. Only by following the roots of I and not-I deep within individual consciousness can men realize the strength and joy that human potential holds in promise. As Lewis Mumford states:

> Man's principal task today is to create a new self, adequate to command the forces that now operate so aimlessly and yet so compulsively. This self will necessarily take as its province the entire world, known and knowable, and will seek, not to impose a

mechanical uniformity, but to bring about an organic unity, based upon the fullest utilization of all the varied resources that both nature and history have revealed to modern man. Such a culture must be nourished, not only by a new vision of the whole, but a new vision of the self capable of understanding and cooperating with the whole. In short, the moment for another great historic transformation has come.[10]

The platform for this "new vision of the self" lies in the next spiral of growth. It is in Spiral V that self-induced advancement meets its fulfillment in the service of mankind.

Humanity is at that crucial point where significant numbers of individuals must outgrow self-centered assertion. As we will see in Spiral V, a pioneering portion of mankind has already made this transition to become more mindful and therefore more patient, more deliberate and therefore more discriminating. They have become tired of the illusions and inflated expectations of upward social mobility and doubtful of the supposed virtues and rewards of modern life. They are quite happy to be more natural and experience the freedom of simplicity. Through detachment from self-centeredness they have expanded consciousness into a profound concern for their fellow beings.

The Free Person

In Spiral V an awareness of inner unity among men signals the end of self-centered assertion. Although the tools of communication remain esthetics and logic, these capabilities are now founded within a more profound center of orientation: the roots of I and not-I have been fused into a perspective where concern for others becomes the foundation for a new way of life. The free person is therefore a man or woman liberated from the prison of self and committed to the service of humanity; he is humanity-oriented and nurtured by an ever-expanding, living warmth for all beings on earth. Within this orientation, self is naturally included in concern for humanity because self is seen as an integrated and living part of humanity and not an entity to be either shunned or worshipped. As expressed by Kohlberg:

> People at this "stage" affirm life from a "cosmic perspective"; feel some mystic union with God, Life, or Nature; and accept the finitude of the self's own life, while finding its meaning in a moral life, a life in which a sense of love for, and union with Life or God is expressed in a love for fellow human beings.[1]

79

One could turn to many traditional sources to establish an overview for the perspective inherent in Spiral V. Hidden within the code languages of Hinduism, Sufism, Taoism, Mahayana Buddhism, Judaism, Christianity, and Platonic philosophy, there is a common core of ideas about continued human growth expressed within the doctrinal context of each epoch. More recent sources illustrate evolved consciousness in terms less obscure to idiosyncrasies of twentieth century thought. From Freud to Jung and Maslow, from Hegel to Whitehead and Teilhard, from Vico to Toynbee and Mumford, our understanding of human development has expanded into a core of knowledge meaningful to modern men.

In developing a picture of Spiral V, it is helpful to start with the idea of "person" developed by Hegel and accented by Teilhard de Chardin. Teilhard is particularly clear about the difference between Individuality and "our person":

> Its (the ego's) only mistake, but a fatal one, is to confuse individuality with personality....The goal of ourselves, and the acme of our originality, is not individuality but our person; and according to the evolutionary structure of the world, we can only find our person by uniting together. There is no mind without synthesis.[2]

Teilhard's distinction is more palatable to traditional Christian theology, of course, because it is focused on the personhood of God. Teilhard is committed to such a conclusion, but evolving individuals, and especially free persons, need not be. For them freedom in part consists of freedom from preestablished intellectual schemes and categorical constraints. Teilhard could be read as an example of a person who attempted to express a more evolved awareness in terms of the language and intellectual structure of a less evolved spiral. Perhaps this is why he has not fully satisfied independent thinkers (who find him compromising) or committed churchmen (who find him subversive). Both groups are right.

One might say that psychology has tended to accept theological language more readily than philosophical discourse as the medium of its insights. This is why it is easier to reformulate concepts of guilt, sin, grace and redemption in psychological language than to translate concepts like Platonic virtue (*arete*), weakness of will (*akrasia*) and pure thought (*noesis*). A few individuals like Erich Fromm and Rollo May stand out as refreshing exceptions to this tendency.

Although Teilhard's progression from individuality to personality is diametrically opposed to traditional philosophic usage, it is neither new nor arbitrary. The word *person* was used by Hegel to describe those men or women who rise above historical limitations; the term *individual* has become tied to the concept of *ego* as an independent self or member of a species. In this vein, recent usage defines a movement from individual to person as a more evolved level of consciousness. But another idea must be added to this distinction before the meaning of the term *free person* is clear—the idea of freedom.

As understood by Rousseau, Kant and Hegel, freedom is more than a synonym for liberty. It represents the Western equivalent of Mahayana Buddhism's "compassion for others transcending all thoughts of self." The status occupied by freedom is emphatically asserted in the following quote from Hegel:

> Freedom alone is the purpose which realizes and fulfills itself, the only enduring pole in the change of

events and conditions, the only truly efficient principle that pervades the whole.[3]

The importance and significance of freedom for Hegel is
undeniable. For the Renaissance philosopher Pico della
Mirandola, freedom is the essential characteristic of
human dignity. In conjunction with ideas like
Rousseau's "General Will," the acid of freedom has been
actively dissolving the brutality of caste, class, and self-
righteous exploitation for at least two centuries. As a
projection of ancient understanding the idea of freedom
embodies an enduring prospect for the institutionaliza-
tion of a just and humane brotherhood among men.

The term *free person* therefore fuses the *person* formulated by Hegel and Teilhard with *freedom*—both in
the sense of liberation from egocentric perspectives and
in the Hegelian idea that one is free only to do what is
right for others. At this level, doing what is right and
what is pleasurable are synthesized, for the free person
takes pleasure in doing what is right.

In considering statements by men who have
undergone the transformation to Spiral V, one invariably encounters the claim to an awareness of human
interdependence. Arthur Koestler, as quoted earlier,
aptly described this awareness as a conviction that "we
were all responsible for each other—not only in the
superficial sense of social responsibility but because, in
some inexplicable manner, we partook of the same
substance of identity, like Siamese twins or communicating vessels." This perspective of underlying
unity among men is grounded in the social adult's sensitivity toward others and the individual capacity for
self-assertion, but the social restrictions that dominate
Spiral III and the psychological separateness that limits
Spiral IV no longer hinder the free person. The result is a

profound liberation of the human capacity for compassionate interaction with others.

The creative strength displayed in the lives of Pascal, Rousseau, and the other men mentioned in the preceding transition, can be further examined through Abraham Maslow's studies of self-actualized people. Because Maslow is one of the very few who have extensively studied post-adult development, his findings are extremely valuable, even though he makes no precise distinctions between mature individuality and higher spirals of growth.

The study of self-actualizing people began with Maslow's interest in two professors whom he admired and respected. His curiosity about these men compelled him to analyze what it was that made them so different. As he thought about them it suddenly struck him that they could be compared through shared characteristics. Growing from this first comparison, Maslow's studies indicated that self-actualizers are more spontaneous and expressive than the average person. They are less emotional, more objective, and have a clearer idea about what is right and wrong. They are also more flexible, courageous, willing to make mistakes, open, and humble in interaction with others. As Maslow states:

> They do not cling to the familiar, nor is their quest for the truth a catastrophic need for certainty, safety, definiteness and order....Thus it comes about that doubt, tentativeness, uncertainty, with the consequent necessity for abeyance of decision, which is for most a torture, can be for some a pleasantly stimulating challenge, a high spot in life rather than a low.[4]

Maslow explains that his subjects are more creative than most people because they have resolved their conflicts and are whole:

> ...the creativity of my subjects seemed to be an epiphenomenon of their greater wholeness and integration, which is what self-acceptance implies. The civil war within the average person between the forces of defense and control seems to have been resolved in my subjects and they are less split. As a consequence, more of themselves is available for use, for enjoyment and for creative purposes. They waste less of their time and energy protecting themselves against themselves.[5]

Anchoring self-actualization in Freudian terms, Maslow writes:

> What I have been describing here may be seen as a fusion of ego, id and super-ego and ego-ideal, of consciousness and unconscious, of primary and secondary processes, of synthesizing of pleasure principle with reality principle,...a true integration of the person at all levels.[6]

While this synthesis appears to describe the apex of human aspiration, Maslow has recognized that self-acceptance seems but a step in the process of human development: "The goal of identity (self-actualization, autonomy, individuation, Horney's real self, authenticity, etc.) seems to be simultaneously an end-goal in itself, and also a transitional goal, a rite of passage, a step along the path to the transcendance of identity."[7] And so it is. Each consolidation of growth is an "end-goal in itself, and also a transitional goal," a resting place in the panorama open to the human mind. Thus Gautama the Buddha, who represents the perfection of human potentiality for awareness to his followers, simultaneously affirmed that he had attained the "terrace of enlightenment" and that he looked to beings who stand in the same relationship to him that he stands in relation to average humanity. Thomas Henry Huxley, the vigorous nineteenth century Darwinist, speculated that evolution implies a potential for human growth so great that one could imagine the humanity of the distant future looking upon present humanity in the way mankind currently looks upon the ant.

Maslow made another crucial observation while describing the inner integrity found in freedom:

> I have the strong intuition that such authentic, fully human persons are the actualization of what many human beings could be. And yet we are confronted with the sad fact that so few people achieve this goal, perhaps only one in a hundred or two hundred.[8]

Considering that "only one in a hundred or two hundred" includes both mature individuals and more evolved spirals of growth, the waste of human potential is indeed a sad fact—not only for the people involved but for society itself. In medicine, social work, business, scientific or academic research, education and all levels of politics there is a great need for the integrated moral and mental capacities found in Spiral V. The alternative is seen everywhere in the accumulation of endless confusion and complexity based on random social values and aggressive self-assertion. For example, efforts to make education rational, interesting, and humane too often degenerate into personality clashes and trivial self-righteousness. While millions of dollars are expended, the integrity of childhood is sacrificed to whirlpools of empty cliches, presumptuous manipulation, and the canons of fiscal efficiency. Such aimless chaos will continue until the compassionate perspective that marks free-person consciousness permeates human endeavor. This does not mean that problems will be magically resolved, but they will become coherent and relevant to human needs in an increasingly complex and interdependent world. Thus the question of why more people do not continue to evolve throughout their lives becomes extremely important.

Part of the answer obviously lies in the Western bias toward individuality and environmental control at the expense of possibilities inherent in the human mind. This tendency is seen not only in psychological efforts that emphasize individual identity as an "end-goal," but in a general preoccupation with only the most evident behavioral aspects of consciousness. Yet there are indications that this bias is being balanced by a more comprehensive perspective. Erik Erikson's work in psychology, for example, is guided by the idea that "personality can be said to develop according to steps predetermined in the human organism's readiness to be driven forward, to be aware of, and to interact with, a widening radius, beginning with the dim image of mother and ending with mankind."[9] Jung made a less tentative assertion about the basis for human growth when he wrote:

> Just as the human body is a museum so to speak of its phylogenetic history, so too is the psyche....the conscious mind cannot be denied a history reaching back at least five thousand years. It is only the ego-consciousness that has forever a new beginning and an early end. The unconscious psyche is not only immensely old, it is also capable of growing into an equally remote future. It moulds the human species and is just as much a part of it as the human body....[10]

The labors of psychologists like Maslow, Erikson, and Jung, as well as of many others in diverse fields, point the way to a more comprehensive perspective of humanity. There is good reason to assume that the inner world of man is as important and as accessible to understanding or direction as the outer world. As Teilhard de Chardin states so beautifully in *The Phenomenon of Man*:

> Man, the center of perspective, is at the same time the *center of construction* of the universe (or world). And by expedience no less than by necessity, all science must be referred back to him. If to see more is really to become more, if deeper vision is really fuller being, then we should look closely at man in order to increase our capacity to live.[11]

Curiously enough, the obstacles to widespread growth into Spiral V arise not only from cultural sources but from characteristics of free persons that warp their relationships with others. Since balanced free persons tend to have environmental relationships differing from esthetic or logical free persons, each group will be considered separately.

Balanced free persons, as described in the last transition, develop through an internal dialectic between esthetics and logic that allows them to bypass much of the intense internal turmoil encountered by others. They less frequently experience the bewildering pain or ecstasy recorded by Tolstoy or Pascal, and they feel no need to develop aggressive or manipulative skills as a means of securing individuality. Because they readily assume that capable people simply grow older and wiser through a process of "letting things happen or by following the golden mean," they are separated from common experience and move easily into absorbing life styles where social interaction is limited to a small circle of friends, students, or associates. Although splendidly "normal" and extremely tolerant, the balanced free person is surprisingly isolated from the social and personal problems faced by most men, a position that may limit his effectiveness as guide or model for those yet to become free.

Esthetic or logical free persons encounter difficulties in relating with social adults and individuals—difficulties which arise from the scope of their perspectives,

the overwhelming depth and intensity of their transformation experiences, and the difficulties inherent in
communication across the chasm of rebirth. A pressing
sense of urgency to communicate the importance of outgrowing limitations can lead to frustration or dead ends.
As with a stranger in a foreign land, great patience is required to relearn the art of listening, to reassess the
aspirations of people, and to integrate a newly formed
organic perspective with shared cultural experience. In
the absence of patience, the common inclination is a
frontal assault upon communication barriers. This is frequently undertaken by focusing upon the trials and
wonder of personal enlightenment as a universal key to
knowledge and understanding. How many free persons
in the full flush of compassion have made the messianic
pronouncement: "I have found the way—have faith and
follow me to the land of light." While a multitude of
cultist and semicultist efforts have helped some across
the threshold, such activities often diffuse the power of
Spiral V consciousness and frequently lead to in-
tolerance and sectarian divisions within humanity. Certainly "a new vision of the self capable of understanding
and cooperation with the whole" contains more than
personal transformation or "salvation" for a chosen
few. The vision that "we are all bound up in one great
tie" may require years of careful thought and preparation before it can become a force for unity among
mankind.

Paradoxically, the inner awareness that awakens one
to the pervasive force and liberating power of compassion often fosters the divisiveness of isolationism,
salvationism, and sectarianism. This is in part due to the
fact that previous spirals involve greater mastery of the
common human inheritance and are efforts to become
fully mature, but with Spiral V, one is moving beyond

maturity as broadly recognized by capable people. Thus one pushes beyond language as used by most human beings. One may begin to forge a new language as Jacob Boehme did, and risk being universally misunderstood or ignored, or attempt to make old symbols bear new meanings and risk giving symbols a psychic weight they cannot bear. Those symbols may taint the individual's vision and thus give rise to a new phenomenon—not so much reversion or regression, but *inversion*.

In spite of such limitations and pitfalls, free-person capabilities have been the leaven for creating a livable world; the long road from capricious tribalism was paved by free-person labors in law, medicine, economic cooperation, and by works of art that link self-consciousness with the majesty of nature. But the road ahead is equally difficult and the burden of pervasive concern for humanity remains heavy.

Occasionally one reaches Spiral V without the crystallization of Spiral IV esthetic and logical capacities. The sensitivity toward others and the desire to do "what's right" that characterizes social adulthood will suddenly expand (usually through an enlightenment experience) into a sense of compassion for others. The result is a simple free person who is devoted to humanity and wants to do only what is right for others, but one who has neither the mental tools nor the self-understanding necessary to fulfill obligations and express insights. When simple free persons find benign refuge, like the naive saints common to monastic environments in the medieval world, they can lead surprisingly productive lives. Brother Leo, favorite companion and disciple of Saint Francis of Assisi, is one of the few relatively well-known examples of these truly gentle yet naive human beings. But when a sanctuary is not found, the result can be dismal. Laboring alone with a burden they cannot bear, many simple free persons live out their lives by weaving frustrated dreams for humanity within cold asylum walls.

The burden of obligation and duty assumed in Spiral V is revealed in this brief look at the simple free person. Yet the mantle of freedom is a source of joy and strength for men or women fully prepared to accept the burden, carry it with dignity and humility, and then pass it on to those they have helped along the path. Moreover, concern for others at the heart of self-consciousness marks the arrival within a brotherhood that—stretching back over the millennia and reaching into the future—labors to actuate the fullest dimensions of the human mind.

By experiencing the exhilaration of what it means to be human, the free person has a profound effect upon those around him. He can relate to many different sorts of people and react to a wide variety of situations with humor and understanding. He displays a shrewd perception of the relationships between means and ends. His creativity allows him to see opportunities where others see in vain. He is so absorbed in what has yet to be tried and yet to be accomplished that there is no time to brood over past achievements and failures. He has emancipated himself from the constrictive prison of self-orientation to enter into the spacious kingdom of humanity. He lives in that dimension of the present which points to the future.

Free Person—Seer Transition

There are two apparent ways to grow beyond Spiral V. The first is the self-induced development of neglected esthetic or logical capacities, an approach that is not at all obvious because counterpart capacities are not necessary for the successful development of Spiral V consciousness. The second way leads to saturation of the dominant capacity by pushing esthetics or logic to the limits of conditional understanding. Then, as Lao Tzu expressed it two and a half millennia ago in the *Tao Te Ching*: "the Yang having reached its extreme retreats in favor of the Yin." After considerable disorientation, counterpart capacities gradually develop. Seen within this framework, wisdom is the synthesis of logic (as thesis) and esthetics (as antithesis), and compassion is the consequent synthesis. Further light might be shed on this process by equating it with synthesis between the hemispheres of the brain where the left lobe (logical, rational, analytic, sequential) is fused with the right (esthetic, intuitive, holistic, simultaneous). In this transition a person steps beyond conditional limitations by fusing esthetic and logical capabilities to reassert the possibility of the reign of compassion and wisdom over the future of life on earth.

There is no way of knowing how many have ventured past the bounds of specific cultural conditions. There are few philosophic sources and no psychological studies to serve as a basis for analysis. Yet the mind's capacity to transcend the limitations imposed by time and circumstance is seen again and again in the lives of men ranging from Gautama Buddha to Saint Francis of Assisi to Albert Einstein. Analysis must proceed by adhering to the logic of dialectic growth, by examining scraps of relevant information wherever found, and by depending upon the few who, in passing this threshold, described the inner process of their development.

A brief look at the life of Albert Schweitzer will help illustrate Spiral V limitations. As a balanced free person well known for his efforts to serve others, Schweitzer was a self-sacrificing giant among men. He saw that the

central problem of modern civilization came down to its
lack of a sense of the sacred—a lack of "reverence for
life." He drew attention to the need for compassion and
intelligence in every interaction with nature or with
other human beings. He was deeply engaged with one of
the central opportunities open to modern man
—technical assistance to those in dire need—and established and maintained a hospital in an impoverished
area of Africa. He publicized the world health problem
and he became a revered figure for others to admire
and follow.

And yet—perhaps because so much thought and experience about aid to technologically underdeveloped
societies has accumulated—deficiencies in his outlook
are starkly evident. Most obvious are the facts that even
his most devoted followers admit: that he sometimes
behaved like an autocratic patriarch, that he was
dogmatically entrenched in nineteenth-century patterns
of thought and action, that the sanitary facilities in his
operating room were inadequate, and that he refused to
install electricity or add tropical medical experts to his
Gabon staff.[12] But beyond these facts, and much more
important to the condition of two-thirds of the world's
population, there is little indication that he had any notion of his own contributions to world chaos. For example, his efforts to curb infant mortality and increase
longevity had an impact on indigenous economic and
social patterns which contributed to local and world
problems. He encouraged the humanitarian idealism of
the nineteenth century through word and deed, but he
did not penetrate immediate African problems. He did
not incorporate or implement an understanding of interrelated organic growth embracing himself, the people
with whom he worked, the African continent, and the
world beyond.

The purpose of this evaluation is not to belabor Schweitzer for not being someone else; it is an attempt to indicate the scope of free person limitations in our modern world. Quite obviously more than mere stubbornness and more than being a "child of his times" is involved in the perceptual limitations of Schweitzer or any other free person. Nor is the search for depth simply a matter of accumulating knowledge, refining technique, or expanding compassion. What is involved in penetrating conditional experience is indicated in a comment made by Einstein relevant to paradoxical contradictions in theoretical physics at the turn of this century:

> Today everyone knows, of course, that all attempts to clarify this paradox satisfactorily were condemned to failure as long as the axiom of the absolute character of time, vis., of simultaneity, *unrecognizedly was anchored in the unconscious.* Clearly to recognize this axiom and its arbitrary character really implies already the solution of the problem.[13] (Emphasis added.)

By exposing what "unrecognizedly was anchored in the unconscious," Einstein created a new superstructure for understanding the physical universe, thereby illustrating the quality of perception capable of providing human endeavor with new depths of purpose and understanding.

Growth beyond Spiral V is based upon a change in the free person's nonself orientation that allows perception beyond conditional experience. What makes this possible? What ingredients within Spiral V provide the impetus for the incredible mentality that synthesizes paradoxes in human understanding? The answers must lie in the power generated between free-person logic and esthetics, for the extension of one factor without the other would produce quantitative rather than qualitative growth. Although esthetic or logical capacities represent partial refinements of the reasoning and intuitive powers latent in the human mind, neither capacity alone is adequate for the perspective embraced by Spiral VI consciousness.

Since growth beyond Spiral V amalgamates a bond between esthetics and logic, one might assume that the balanced free person is most likely to achieve further growth. But this is unlikely because the balanced free person's absorption in the richness of his internal life, together with the absence of an intense qualifying struggle in attaining freedom, would appear to preclude the possibility of qualitative development. Although the balanced free person is significant as a stabilizing force in society, he apparently lacks the internal dynamism or motivation necessary to reach Spiral VI. The free person with a predominance of either esthetic or logical capabilities would seem more likely to transcend Spiral V limitations. The superficial observer might think that those with greatest internal tension rise highest in the spirals of growth, but this is not true. Tension may stimulate awareness of the need to seek resolution, but in itself tension—both psychic and social—is destructive. Rather, growing individuals must be wary of premature synthesis, the ability to achieve an inwardly harmonious life at a level far below ultimate human potential. Those for whom each synthesis is seen as a doorway to greater possibilities are drawn on to explore them. Though they seek balance, they do not fear disequilibrium, for they find settling for less than what is possible inherently unsatisfactory. Thus a balanced person may choose to tip the scales, a sure sign of an individual in quest of new levels of consciousness.

In portraying the drama of unfolding consciousness,

it will be helpful to review salient points in esthetic or logical development before the unfolding of Spiral VI consciousness is explored. Esthetic or logical individuals evolve by synthesizing contradictions within either an esthetic or logical framework. Thus the logical individual usually retains social-adult emotions and becomes a free person by virtue of contradictions wholly within a logical structure of perception. The esthetic individual operates with social-adult reason to become a free person by developing contradictions within an esthetic framework. Thus the logical or esthetic free person has largely undeveloped emotional or reasoning capacities that are not troublesome due to Spiral V self-awareness. It is worth remembering that the self-awareness of the logical or esthetic free person has been tempered by the fires of many battles lost and won.

In a person who develops esthetics or logic to the limits, the saturation of one capacity can provoke disruptive mental phenomena, a fear-evoking and highly disorienting Spiral VI illumination. An excellent description of this experience was written by Henri Michaux, a contemporary author who was awarded the 1964 Nobel Prize for literature. Describing one who is experiencing an expansion of consciousness, he says:

> He receives a constant, enormous, unknown secretion, in every sense, which he could have never conceived, of an ampleness which is beyond him, of a scope which uplifts him, which nothing could express, of a fantastic measurelessness beyond all comparison. That is what he feels, what he felt, for each moment this sentiment takes on a fabulous increase, an increase that cannot be satisfied. A fan-wise expansion, not fan-wise, sphere-wise, dilating, which dilates further, which dilates to the maximum, and yet after that dilates still more and must ever magnify itself more, lend itself to a greater plenitude,

offer itself to the invisible plowshare that plows his
being with a view to the new, to an immensely large
opening. . . . this "immensity," "this too-muchness,"
cannot continue thus. Yet it continues on and
on. . . . Coexistent immense. What immense? There is
missing a head to this enormous gestation. . . .[14]

To understand the significance of this kind of illumination the entire range of enlightenment experiences must
be explored.

While this is venturing where angels fear to tread, it
is necessary to gain a tentative perspective on the
multiplicity of enlightenment experience. Some are
structured around a specific content such as Teilhard's
vision of Christ, and others are diffuse like the expanding flux described by Michaux. Mahayana Buddhist
doctrines provide a framework for dividing enlightenment experiences into three categories: "conditional or
imperfect," "unconditional or perfect," and "unlocalized
or absolute."[15] While it is impossible to know precisely
what the ancient Buddhists had in mind without
experiencing these forms oneself, or even if the
English translation captures the intended meaning,
the qualitative distinctions between *conditional*, *unconditional*, and *unlocalized* can be understood in terms
relevant to spirals of growth.

Conditional enlightenment is bound up with the
transformation to Spiral V in which internal reorganization stems from the conditional experience of esthetic or
logical individuals as they probe the roots of I and not-I
in both personal and social life. Thus the visions of
Pascal and Teilhard were organized around the idea or
figure of Christ, Rousseau's around institutional reform,
and Koestler's around humanity. Unconditional
enlightenment experiences are related to growth into
Spiral VI and unlocalized or absolute illuminations to

growth beyond Spiral VI. Since growth beyond Spiral
VI will be considered later, we can focus on unconditional enlightenment experiences as they affect the
transition to Spiral VI.

Since the transition to Spiral VI is concerned with
penetrating the limitations of conditional experience—with overcoming the preconceptions that bind
perception and conception—unconditional enlightenment experiences are related to growth toward Spiral
VI. But, as indicated before, such experiences can be extremely disorienting. For example, the great logician
Saint Thomas Aquinas was apparently overwhelmed by
an unconditional illumination while deeply involved in
his *Summa Theologia*. Joseph Campbell has described
the effects of this experience in *The Hero with a Thousand Faces*:

> Thomas Aquinas, as the result of a mystical ex-
> perience while celebrating mass in Naples, put his
> pen and ink on the shelf and left the last chapters of
> his *Summa Theologia* to be completed by another
> hand. "My writing days," he stated, "are over,
> for such things have been revealed to me, that all I
> have written and taught seems of small account
> to me, wherefore I hope in my God that, even as the
> end has come to my teaching, so it may soon come in
> my life." Shortly thereafter, in his forty-ninth year,
> he died.[16]

An observer whose own conscious life is best described by Spiral IV or V might well see Aquinas's revelation and subsequent response as a kind of life failure.
There is no good evidence to believe Aquinas thought
so. The artist leaves the completed canvas for others to
admire while he pushes on to new creative expression.
What others might call his lifework, Aquinas could see
as only a preparation for the illumination in Naples.

While unconditional experiences can be overwhelming, they are not random, unstructured, or meaningless. Aquinas indicates that "such things have been revealed to me;" and even Michaux's vision, although "missing a head to this enormous gestation," was characterized by energy and expansion. Another reaction to unconditional illumination also accompanied by fear, was recorded by Albert Einstein:

> This insight into the mystery of life, coupled though it be with fear, has also given rise to religion. To know [that] what is impenetrable to us really exists, manifesting itself as the highest wisdom and the most radiant beauty which our dull faculties can comprehend only in their most primitive forms—this knowledge, this feeling, is at the center of true religiousness. In this sense, and in this sense only, I belong in the ranks of devoutly religious men....It is enough for me to contemplate the mystery of conscious life perpetuating itself through all eternity, to reflect upon the marvelous structure of the universe which we dimly perceive, and to try humbly to comprehend even an infinitesimal part of the intelligence manifest in nature.[17]

These examples point to a characteristic of illumination that must be unraveled before the subject can be considered as anything but an interesting mental phenomenon. While any level of illumination is potentially reorienting and disorienting, this is particularly true of the unconditional experience that destroys or severely alters concepts of time, space, subject, object, God, love, and all conditional categories by which the human mind normally organizes perception. The problem to consider is why illumination experiences can be either a magnet for further growth or a cul-de-sac of the mind, and why these experiences are consistently recorded as crucially important in people's lives. Why do they drive some men insane, cause others (like Aquinas) to lose interest in life, and stimulate still others to further growth? An apparent answer to these questions is that, although an illumination penetrates a higher spiral of consciousness, it by no means insures that the vision can be absorbed or incorporated for further growth. In other words, an enlightenment of whatever type—conditional, unconditional, or unlocalized—is something like a mental short circuit that unfolds an instantaneous picture of the organizing principle within a more evolved spiral of growth. Whether the experience is benign or destructive appears to depend upon other factors. It is parallel to the anthropological concept of "rites of passage" (originally applied to birth, marriage and death, and extended to entering and leaving social units and a whole range of phenomena) which has exactly this meaning: the passage through a transition phase, a threshold or a nexus at which the outcome is uncertain. While the anthropological notion focuses on *horizontal* transitions (changes within one level of consciousness), enlightment experiences mark *vertical* transitions (changes from one spiral of consciousness to another).

Among the most important factors influencing the results of an illumination experience is timing. Other than the dialectical tension between spirals of growth, illuminations can be triggered by internal or external shock, illness, emotional crisis, drugs, and starvation. Thus an individual can have a conditional enlightenment that paves the way to Spiral V, but the same experience could be overwhelming during the transition to Spiral III. Perceiving more than one is equipped to digest can lead to hysteria, suicide, years of internal ambivalence, existence in an oddly structured visionary world, or the jumps in growth considered in each of the preceeding spirals. Even when the experience occurs at the most appropriate time, the process of comprehending, integrating, and utilizing the insight requires sustained effort and self-control.

While there may be other ways to integrate an unconditional enlightenment, the obvious approach is through a dialectic between esthetics and logic. One should notice that throughout the preceding discussion, only the most vivid and obvious illumination experiences have been considered. Yet it is quite possible that rather than one explosive flash, there can be a series of lesser experiences or insights that gradually light the way ahead. The mind seems to reach within itself to find direction either gradually or suddenly. Teilhard, for example, had a conditional illumination that opened the way to Spiral V, yet years later while deep in transition to Spiral VI, he spoke of the "terror of falling back into the energies of the cosmos." This comment precisely echoes the unconditional experiences described by Michaux and Einstein, but there is no evidence that the paleontologist/priest had an unconditional enlightenment. Instead, his comment indicates a struggle to assimilate the unconditional awareness that accompanies growth into Spiral VI. Illuminations are not doors but windows to more refined realms of perception. They must be followed by extensive reconstruction of both knowledge and self-awareness before new forms of understanding can be assimilated and communicated to other men. What must be given up as well as what might be gained affects the process of assimilation.

The continuing interplay between illuminations, knowledge, and self-awareness can be clarified by following the efforts of esthetic and logical men who have stripped consciousness of conditional props to pave the way to Spiral VI.

The life of poet Allen Ginsberg exemplifies the relevance of esthetic free persons in the modern world, and it also illustrates the difficulties encountered in developing the luminous counterparts that lead to more evolved perception. Living in New York as "poet-prophet on the side of love and wild good," Ginsberg experienced a peak experience at age twenty-two:

> And one day, while lying by an open window on a couch, reading Blake, my eye fell on the printed page, and suddenly I heard a voice pronouncing the words on the page—Blake's *Sun Flower*....And simultaneously I was having an illumination, very similar to some aspects of the illumination you get with the psychedelic drugs—except deeper, more ample, more real and blissful than anything I've experienced since. Everything around me seemed completely alive, like a concretized intelligence, so that looking out of the window, all the cornices, the Victorian cornices of 1910 apartment houses of Spanish Harlem slums, they all became the handiwork of a creator—every brick and on up into the sky, the sun, the very blue substance of space.[18]

This experience was followed by seven years of interplay between the harmony revealed by his vision and self-evaluation in which Ginsberg gradually consolidated consciousness characteristic of the esthetic individual. In 1955 the assertion of individuality was marked by a sudden resolve to "quit my job, my tie and suit, and go off and do what I wanted." In Ginsberg's case this meant assuming responsibility for the anguish of a creative generation as embodied in his poem "Howl."

Still operating with social adult reason, Ginsberg's first reaction to self-orientation was to stop writing and become publicist and spokesman for the "beat" literary genre. The limits of this approach were expressed by his friend Jack Kerouac who described Ginsberg as a "hairy loss" to the beat literary world. To resolve the conflict between ends and means, Ginsberg began a world pilgrimage. After years of travel, a new answer crystallized:

> It came to me, everything at once, in a moment of great euphoric weeping. I saw the end to the moral necessity to enlarge my being, that I could just be myself as I am, now me, to live in this form as a human being now. The whole visionary game was lost to me. I was alive in a body that was going to die. Then I began looking around the train and seeing all the other mortal faces—faces of weakness and woe, as Blake has it, and I saw how exquisitely dear they all were. Unique and frail, each a thing about to die.

In rejecting the "visionary game" it would appear that Ginsberg had evolved from a "beat" poet into a humanitarian author concerned with the welfare of others. Returning to America he ceaselessly implored others to open themselves to more human life values. His personal integration of ends and means in iconoclastic activity and humanitarian thought would seem to illustrate the powerful integrity of free-person consciousness operating within the framework of modern society.

It is fortunate that Ginsberg relaxed his tight esthetic grip in concern for others. Otherwise, unrelieved esthetic tension may have degenerated into the utter despair for humanity depicted in Kafka's novels and Goya's later paintings. But the full development of counterpart logic is another question, perhaps more difficult for a poet than any other artist, due to dependence upon spontaneous insight. Years of concentrated effort would be necessary to develop a systematic logical capacity, a task perhaps accomplished only by artists of the stature of Goethe and Shakespeare.

Developing and maintaining the momentum necessary to contain unconditional insight is difficult even for the logical free person. However, he does have an advantage over the esthetic free person due to the systematic character of his mind, at least in Western societies where science and philosophy unfold dilemmas within a logical framework. The life of the seventeenth-century scientist and thinker Pascal illustrates the process of logical free-person expansion and growth. As previously described, Pascal's logical individuality was shattered by a conditional enlightenment during the "night of fire." Subsequent to this experience he turned most of his attention from seventeenth-century science to institutional and moral problems. With the assumption of free-person responsibility, he wrote the polemical *Provinciales* letters in an attempt to expand moral and religious understanding. His efforts in science and moral philosophy soon encountered the limits of seventeenth-century conditional knowledge, while polemical writing developed his esthetic capacity. Pushing himself despite obstacles, he precipitated a transitional crisis that lasted six years until his death. Lucien Goldmann's study on Pascal described the dialectical roots of this transitional crisis:

> Pascal himself marked the beginning of the crisis. . . when he wrote in 1657, these words whose accuracy and controlled power make them some of the most shattering ever penned by a believer who still looked upon himself as belonging to a religion and church: "the anguish of seeing oneself torn between the Pope and the Church." When their implications were finally developed, these words led to the manuscript of the *Pensées*.[19]

The *Pensées* is a particularly interesting document because it reflects Pascal's efforts to recognize the past-future continuum of human values while remaining true to his esthetic vision and logical observations of religion, himself, and society. Attempting to bridge the seventeenth-century gap between growing secular awareness and shrinking religious values, Pascal produced a juxtaposition of opposites where "the only answer to every problem is both Yes and No, and paradox is the only valid expression of reality."[20] In readjusting his mind to the changing human needs, he was caught between personal "reasons of the heart that reason does not know" and logical observations—a conflict that Goldmann sums up as familiar to both Kant and Pascal:

> For both thinkers the physical universe—together with everything that can be known on the theoretical plane of reason in Pascal, or in the understanding of Kant—has ceased to present the existence of God as either certain or probable. There is no physical or ontological proof of His existence, and the famous proposition by which Kant summed up his own position—"I have had to abolish knowledge in order to make room for faith"—is also an exact description of the conclusion of the *Pensées*.[21]

In addition to his inner struggles, Pascal labored for others to the end of his life. For example, he organized the first cheap public transportation service to help the poor and donated the profits to charity. Pascal died before an unconditional synthesis could resolve the dilemma between knowledge and faith, but his struggle is a beautiful example of the self-conscious efforts necessary to attain Spiral VI.

What follows is the life of a man who did achieve the synthesis and was unusually clear about the step-by-step process of his development.

Teilhard de Chardin was born in 1881, the fourth of eleven children, and spent his childhood in the heart of France's Massif Central where the rich mountain environment, together with understanding, religious parents, evoked a lifelong preoccupation with nature and Christianity. Becoming a Jesuit novitiate, he pursued this dual interest as a student of geology and paleontology, theology and philosophy, to become a science teacher at the Jesuit college in Cairo. Just before his ordination as priest in 1911, his logical individuality was crystallized by reading Henri Bergson's *Creative Evolution*.[22] This book, representing the culmination of early twentieth-century evolutionary thought, provided a basis for intellectual labors throughout his life. It is interesting to note that the importance of outgrowing social-adult dualisms is reflected in a comment made nearly forty years after this exposure: "I was thirty when I abandoned the antiquated static dualism and emerged into a universe in process of guided evolution. What an intellectual revolution!"[23]

Teilhard's logical labors were interrupted by World War I where he served with distinction as a stretcher bearer on the western front. Forced absence from rigorous intellectual work, together with emersion in the nightmare of trench warfare, evidently provoked dilemmas resolved through a spectacular vision of Christ:

> The first thing I noticed was that the vibrant atmosphere which surrounded Christ with a halo was not confined to the small sphere immediately about him, but that it radiated to infinity. It was shot through from time to time by what appeared to be phosphorescent trails, tracing a continuous path of light as far as the outermost spheres of matter—making a sort of plexis of blood vessels or networks of

nerves throughout all substance.

The whole universe vibrated. And yet when I tried
to look at things one by one, I found them still as
clearly defined, their individuality still
preserved....What is certain is that these in-
numerable shades of majesty, of gentleness, of ir-
resistible attraction, succeeded each other, were
transformed and merged into each other with a harmony which appeased me to the full.[24]

The conditional vision of Christ as a benevolent unity
animating and pervading the universe both inspired and
delimited all his subsequent work. Teilhard never
outgrew the specific "Christification" revealed by his
vision—never saw it as a "conditional or imperfect"
enlightenment steeped in his Jesuit-Catholic fund of
personal experience.

Soon after his conditional illumination, his letters
began to reflect the free-person sense of moral responsibility toward humanity. "I think," he wrote during the
winter of 1918-1919, "this real solidarity of humanity is
a fact that is only being slowly apprehended, that it is an
idea that we who have come to realize it have to assist in
thinking into the collective mind."[25] The perception that
the "solidarity of humanity" is a concrete reality, a fact
rather than a dream, is a superb example of free-person
orientation in the service of mankind.

But insights of this order become socially relevant
through communication, or, as Teilhard put it, after
they have been "thought into the collective mind." At
this point in his life, Teilhard faced the problem of
communication across the chasm of rebirth, a problem
he noted by stating:

I sometimes feel myself overcome by my powerless-
ness to make others see....Where can one find the
souls who have vision? How can one bring them into

> being and associate (i.e., unite) them, hampered as
> we are by the countless ties and associations of
> modern conventions and regulations.[26]

In Teilhard's case the need to transmit ideas necessitated the development of esthetic capabilities that would complement his logical capacity.

Teilhard's first attempt in the esthetic realm was *The Divine Milieu*, completed in 1927, which presented his vision of human unity "in the form of a prayer." Although esthetically complete, the book was no answer to the problem of communication: it was suppressed by his ecclesiastical superiors and was intellectually immature in comparison to his subsequent works. As he himself stated many years later:

> Today when I re-read the frankly fervent pages of the
> *Milieu Divin*, I am amazed to discover the extent to
> which the essential features of Christo-Cosmic vision
> were already determined. But, on the other hand,
> I am surprised to see how vague and fluctuating my
> conception of the Universe was at this time...[27]

Work on *The Divine Milieu* brought his logical and esthetic capacities into balance, and the long search for underlying order, unity, and purpose between paleontology and religion began. In fact, the process that eventually forges Spiral VI awareness began in 1927 before *The Divine Milieu* was finished:

> I propose to undertake a study of Man, not just
> prehistoric Man, but Man as the greatest telluric and
> biological event on our planet. I am more and more
> convinced that we are as blind to the terrestrial layer
> of man as our forefathers were to the mountains and
> oceans...geology extends into the human, and it is
> this prolongation that we have to bring out.[28]

Culmination of this study came in 1947 with *The*

Phenomenon of Man. But between intent and fulfillment lay years of sequential consolidation which sheds
considerable light on the process of deepening perception beyond conditional experience. The first step in this
process was "universalism" in which Teilhard learned to
reason from an inclusive perception of unity to particulars in his life and work. This was followed six years
later by "futurism"; and finally these two insights were
blended with a third synthesis called "personalism."

The first step to universalism began with a "little
crisis." Teilhard was removed from the Institut catho-
lique in Paris, where he desired to work, and sent to
China. Here he encountered the masses of humanity, the
very vastness of China, removal from familiar academic
and religious routine, and the intellectual excitement
surrounding the discovery of Peking Man. All this provoked years of intensive self-examination. Eventually
Teilhard came to the realization that the exploration of
the past must proceed from an appreciation for the continuing unity of life. Behind this realization, he had
evolved to see himself as part of a process which he
called universalism. Describing his reaction to this
insight, Teilhard wrote:

> I have the curious feeling of having lost the faculty of
> enjoying (or wishing) anything whatsoever in con-
> nection with myself; at the same time the supreme
> grandeur of the destiny of the universe, a business in
> which we are all engaged by the very fact of our
> existence, dominates me continually.[29]

With the conditional limitations of freedom outgrown
through intimate identification with a sweeping perception of unity, he began a reevaluation of paleontology.
The painful question (especially for a paleontologist)
was how to consider the past when it is the future that
demands attention. Teilhard's deceptively simple syn-

thesis was that the past is important only as far as it reveals "how the future is built":

> It is almost as though, for reasons arising from the progress of my science, the past and its discovery had ceased to interest me. The past has revealed to me how the future is built and preoccupation with the future tends to sweep everything else aside.... It's perfectly simple, but there are still so many people who behave as though the past was interesting in itself, and treat it as only the future deserves to be treated.[30]

Here one can see how one's cultural milieu affects the problems one must solve. Had Teilhard grown up in a Hindu or Buddhist environment, he would have encountered the doctrine of *karma* or universal causation. He would have grown up with the idea that the whole past is inherent in the configuration of the present, as a cause is inherent in the effect, and that the present prefigures the future. This is not mechanistic determinism, but rather causation extended to the mental and moral realms as well as physical nature. Thus the doctrine of *karma* has been called "the law of ethical causation."

Universalism and futurism, are master insights synthesized from a long period of work in China. They represent the results of the persistent "groping, fumbling, tentative efforts" that Oppenheimer described as leading to scientific breakthrough where "error may give way to less error, confusion to less confusion, and bewilderment to insight." That Teilhard's integration came first in science is hardly surprising since, in recent Western history, science has become a cauldron for collective insight. But he went further. As Oppenheimer has implored of all science, the French Jesuit successfully integrated morality with paleontology and then radiated the synthesis into the realm of man's ethical life. This he accomplished through a specifically Christian synthesis called "personalism" in which he blended the joyously universal with the deepening sensitivity of his internal life.

> Never before perhaps did I perceive so clearly the possible meaning of the evolution of my internal life: the dark purple of universal matter, first passing for me into the gold of spirit, then into the white incandescence of personality, then finally (and this is my present stage) into the immaterial (or rather supermaterial) ardor of love.[31]

Years of relentless exploration in paleontology and religion were integrated into a sweeping continuity of self, past, and future. Love of God was no longer an interrelationship between man and the summit of the world, but the authority through which the world or universe becomes one evolving unity. Unlike Kant and Pascal, he did not "abolish knowledge in order to make room for faith," but created a synthesis of the religious-scientific dilemmas that had tortured these men. Within the vast dimensions of geologic time Teilhard had uncovered an answer to the significance of human life: faith-God-immensity were blended with knowledge-man-earth in a life-God continuum of growth. In Teilhard's eyes "co-reflection" had forged humanity into the equivalent of a new "type" of evolutionary organism capable of guiding world destiny toward final convergence with God, a "Point Omega." Against chaos or entropy (i.e., "the terror of falling back into the energies of the cosmos"), the ardor of love or universal compassion crystallizes the strength that makes things one without direction.[32] The dark night of the soul was over. Teilhard had arrived at Spiral VI.

Up to this point we have explored the struggles of the

esthetic and logical free persons as they prepare for and grow beyond Spiral V. While the interplay between illumination, insight, and personal experience should now be reasonably clear, what remains obscure is the difference between conditional and unconditional perception. To demonstrate the power of insight that penetrates the limitations imposed by time and circumstance, a crucial aspect of Teilhard's mature work will be explored for its significance in the modern world.

From 1937 through completion of the *The Phenomenon of Man* to his death in 1955, Teilhard unfolded the organic unity of his ideas while actively maintaining his position as one of the world's most distinguished paleontologists. He worked from empirical evidence which indicates that man is an unfinished and evolving being whose latent potentialities are becoming active. He devoted himself to outlining the process whereby evolution, becoming conscious of itself through thinking humanity, might take possession of its own forces in conjunction with a revised Christian perspective of God. The extent of the revolutionary changes he contemplated is illustrated in a letter dated April 28, 1954:

> We have been forced to abandon the static Aristotelian cosmos and have been introduced (through the whole modern physico-chemical-biological system) into a universe still in a state of cosmogenesis. In the future, therefore, we have to rethink our Christology in terms of Christogenesis (at the same time as we rethink our anthropology in terms of anthropogenesis.) And such an operation is not simply a matter of slight readjustment of certain aspects. As a result of the introduction of a new dimension, the whole thing has to be recast (just as when you move from plane to spherical geometry)—a tremendous effort: and from it, I assure you, Christ will emerge in triumph, the savior of anthropogenesis.[33]

One can see why the ecclesiastical authorities condemned Teilhard's work. He sought to transmute Christian doctrine; they saw that he would take it out of their control. Although he considered his insights as an "unquestionably Christian point of view," his religious superiors prevented the publication of all his controversial or major works during his lifetime. Bursting with a vital, prophetic message, and the responsibility of Freedom, this treatment frequently drove Teilhard to the verge of total despair, particularly during the latter years of his life.[34]

The specific Christian cast of Teilhard's conclusions make them awkward and sometimes unintelligible to secular scholars. However, the very strangeness of terminology, coupled with his work in modern science, indicates limits and strength important to an understanding of unconditional but localized perception. Spiral VI perception is apparently localized within specific realms of knowledge. Nevertheless there is always an unconditional element in visionary insight which transcends the particulars of personal integration to illuminate fundamentals in the human condition. Men still turn to Plato, bow quietly to Lao-Tsu, marvel at Saint Francis, and read Jeremiah. The integrity of these men as humans, together with the inclusiveness of their vision, radiates across the ages.

Teilhard's perception was localized in that it focused on evolution as the unifying factor between Christianity and paleontology. The scope of his perception allowed an expansion of Julian Huxley's formulation that "man is evolution become conscious of itself" until the idea became as inclusive and potent as $E=MC^2$. Just as Einstein's formula necessitated rethinking not only the fundamentals of physics but the exercise of physical power in all its social and political dimensions, the same sweeping necessity applies to Chardin's break-through—as he was himself aware. In hurling the insight upon us, Chardin observed that "we must rethink our anthropology in terms of anthropogenesis. And such an operation is not simply a matter of slight readjustment of certain aspects."

It follows that we must eventually rethink nearly every area of intellectual endeavor relative to the study of man. The phylum of evolution would include the areas of geology, paleontology, archeology, anthropology, history, psychology, sociology and economics. The Teilhard-Julian Huxley idea that "man is evolution become conscious of itself" integrates each of these structurally isolated disciplines into a panorama of interacting thought. The study of history, for example, would lose much of its arbitrariness of conception and narrow institutionalism as well as its penchant for nationalistic ethnocentrism and particularist obsessions with the past. At the same time the value of history—whether concerned with ancient Mesopotamia, eleventh-century China, or modern France—becomes deeply germane and relevant as a record and analysis of human experiments in self-consciousness. From breakthrough and failure to over-success and rigidity, history is a record of man's precarious struggles as evolution becomes self-consciously aware of itself. The same integrative process is possible in every social-science discipline.

Like the work of Einstein, Teilhard's mature thought resolves a morass of conditional limitations by providing guidelines for restructuring human endeavor. Surely the future rests on encouraging the growth of more men with this level of perception, particularly at a time in history when human technological advancements and nuclear proliferation threaten to destroy the life balance of an evolutionary progression stretching back millions of years. It is almost as if destiny were holding its breath, watching a precarious metamorphosis as evolution transcends the blind impulse to become responsibly conscious of itself through humanity.

The answer to creating the mentality that sees beyond the limitations in time and circumstance can only lie in developing the resources inherent in the human mind. The same hundred-million cell complex that acted in conjunction with others of its kind to produce our technological civilization is more than capable of integrating capacity with purpose (*is* with *ought*) and capability with direction (*can* with *should*). And even though the birth of modern civilization has produced hazards and perils, it has also created a cultural mind-set devoted to the systematic accumulation and use of knowledge about ourselves and our environment. If this mind-set is given adequate direction through the cultivation of Spiral VI consciousness, man will soon assume his position as responsible agency for the organic complex of life on earth.

Spiral VI

The Seer

Spiral VI represents the seer level of comprehensive engagement that penetrates the core of contemporary knowledge to integrate and direct particular modes of human life. Wisdom or compassion brought to the roots of understanding is the center of orientation. A seer, meaning one who "sees," is able to perceive the unity behind contradictions in specific structures of human expression or knowledge. The time-honored concept of seer has been reduced in recent centuries to the notion of a clairvoyant by many who take that idea seriously, and to that of a card reader or charlatan by those who jeer at it. Here we invoke the ancient concept of one who sees clearly, one for whom empirical space and clock time are not binding limitations, but whose depth of understanding, eye for essentials, and awareness of causality permits one to read the future like an open book and to observe what passes in the hearts of men.[1] They can, therefore, unfold radical new vistas of order and unity, harmony and purpose to stimulate the growth of conscious life. As explained by Raghavan Iyer in *Parapolitics*:

> Wisdom involves the continual expansion of
> awareness of alternatives, the development of an eye
> for essentials. Wisdom is needed to penetrate the core
> of anything—of a situation, of reality, of a problem.
> The discriminating eye focuses like a laser beam, so
> concentrated, intense, and powerful that in penetrat-
> ing the core it burns out irrelevant obscurations. It
> removes mental blinders, linking all in a collective
> awareness.[2]

A portrait of the seer would reflect the wisdom or compassion of his perceptions. He is persistent through
struggle and pain, through error and imperfection. His
desires and needs are minimal, tastes simple, posture
humble. He is flexible in perspective and in the formulation of what is necessary and what may be possible. An
aura of warm and direct innocence is permeated by both
sweeping concern and detachment. Think of Plato, Lao-
Tzu, Saint Francis, Dante, Spinoza, Teilhard—what a
montage of extraordinary human beings! And what a
hope they represent for the future of man, not only for
the heritage they provide but as mentors for the
possibilities of the human mind.

Spiral VI insight is "pure" in that it accrues beyond
any specific esthetic and logical framework of communication. But insight is still bound to society in two
ways: it must be translated into terminology others can
understand and use; and insight is the result of a dialectic between the seer's awareness of what it means to
be human and problems that come to light at the core
of structured knowledge. Because Spiral VI insight
incorporates compassion for life into the growth of
knowledge-structures, it is necessary to understand how
knowledge-structures relate to particular historic circumstances before the significance of the seer can be
fully grasped.

Bodies of knowledge such as economics, politics, military organizations, and the natural sciences can be defined as systematic and cumulative responses to classes of problems within a society. While what we call religion, art, economics, and politics are blended within one integral structure in simple societies, the knowledge-structures within a complex society, almost by definition, have separate traditions and different effects upon the whole. In most complex societies the balance between knowledge-structures is constantly shifting, giving different casts to rather distinct historical eras.

Because bodies of knowledge are historic reservoirs for ordering knowledge and communicating insight, they also isolate and juxtapose the dialectic problems through which human consciousness struggles for expansion and growth. In other words, they are areas of accumulative endeavor through which people as well as ideas grow. Therefore the quality of insight that dominates systems of knowledge is crucially important in determining what people believe, what they are willing to do, and how they evolve as human beings.

Since knowledge arises from seer-level insight rooted in compassion, it follows that such knowledge should incorporate a sense of human responsibility. Yet even a cursory glance reveals that bodies of knowledge are frequently directed by sweeping insights that are not rooted in a sense of compassion. Thermo-nuclear weapons, along with the economic, military, and religious refinements of nations such as Phoenicia, Sparta, and ancient Egypt, are as inhumane as they are brilliant. Evidently, knowledge can grow through a type of seer insight that does not incorporate a sense of compassion for others. It is apparent, too, that morally irresponsible knowledge can proliferate to threaten and even destroy an entire civilization.

It seems that there is a type of seer who does not integrate the free person sense of moral duty and obligation toward others, but jumps directly from individuality to Spiral VI. Developed people of this type—methodological seers—provide new frameworks for knowledge that eventually corrupt the evolution of human endeavor. Methodological insight is not true seership because it depends upon technique, not vision—that is, the capacity to develop and channel power rather than to share insights. Because methodological seers present serious problems for the future, analysis of Spiral VI consciousness will proceed by exploring the differences between them and true seers.

For approximately five thousand years, men and women of authentic insight have employed several procedures to cope with noncompassionate knowledge and to insure that the power inherent in Spiral VI insight was not abused. "Mysteries" like the Chinese *I Ching* and the Greek Elusinian Mysteries, or codes for developing insight like Saint Bernard's Mystic Ladder of Love or Zen Buddhism, were designed to foment growth beyond individuality. In conjunction with codes and mysteries, various forms of discipleship compelled sensitive young people to accept guidance in growing slowly and completely through successive spirals of awareness. Elaborate precautions insured that potentially destructive knowledge was shrouded in obscurity or hidden from those outside the community of initiates. The ancient wise men, seers, did not condone knowledge as an end in itself because they well understood that knowledge was power and could produce disastrous personal and social consequences. They centered their efforts upon creating and preserving islands of human transcendence that would survive resurgent tides of misery and social chaos. Brotherhoods and monastic communities, mysteries and codes, obscure knowledge and discipleship, religious and philosophic cults—all these were utilized in various combinations to assure the probability that a few individuals would develop under guidance. These institutions also insured that knowledge would evolve through future insights firmly anchored in a comprehensive engagement with life.

The old seer programs were never completely successful because there were always brilliant, sensitive, and tenacious individuals who did not develop under their aegis. Moreover, and of crucial importance, there were always methodological opportunities for the development of Spiral VI insight that did not require the highest knowledge. Opportunity beckoned wherever evolved bodies of knowledge reduced complex social interrelationships to precisely delineated problems and at the same time provided methodological tools for analysis. Structures like hierarchical religions, political organizations, military establishments, and centralized economies furnished both the deeply absorbing challenges and the methodological tools that enabled gifted young individuals to penetrate the core of specific kinds of knowledge. Seer insight was open to brilliant young men through such channels, but premature dedication to the absorbing rigors of structural analysis caused them to bypass growth through the humane dimensions of Spiral V self-consciousness. An illustration can be taken from the traditional history of the Kabbalah. After the destruction of the Second Temple in Jerusalem, it is said that Simeon ben Jochai took the decision to write down some of the teachings of the Kabbalah, the secret teaching of mystical Judaism. The choice was difficult because written teachings are subject to misunderstanding and to being stolen by those unprepared to make proper use of them. With the loss of

the Temple, however, Simeon feared that the core group
of initiates would be dispersed and the teachings lost.
This story shows the value of institutions—in this case,
the Temple and writing—and also the dangers that use
of institutions pose to Spiral VI consciousness.

There have always been individuals of methodological insight, and the old devices that limited their
numbers worked reasonably well until approximately
the fifteenth century. After that, the Renaissance gave
impetus to manipulative individualism; Protestant personalism broke down master-disciple relations; the rise
of skepticism destroyed the allure of mystery;
bureaucracies began to proliferate; and power replaced
transcendence as the focus of intellectual attainment.
Drawn by this tide, gifted men increasingly rejected
"mysterious" doctrines, eschewed communal
discipleship, and pursued knowledge and environmental
control as ends in themselves. These blows to the ancient insight tradition were all distortions and abuses of
Renaissance, Reformation, and early scientific perspectives.

As interplay intensified between mind and machine,
number and fact, system and control, the focus of
evolutionary consciousness gradually shifted to reveal a
fresh new world resplendent with promise but riddled
with peril. Dreams became "earth centered" as the
source of human inspiration shifted from other-worldly
perfection to the manipulation and control of nature.
The New Kingdom began to rise in concrete and plastic
splendor: misery was alleviated in favored parts of the
world, the length and material quality of life increased,
and the shackles of economic bondage began to dissolve. Yet men of great insight like His Holiness, the
fourteenth Dalai Lama have argued that modern man is
subject to greater spiritual bondage and psychological

misery than ever before.

Knowledge was unleashed and methodology enthroned while the codes and communities of the old order lay scattered and scorned—and with them the far-seeing humanity of deep seer vision. A Pascal or Spinoza could agonize over the tragic loss, but lamentation lacks persuasive power where opportunity abounds. Whether impelled by a vision as was Descartes, by the sheer mental capacity of Newton and Teller, or by the "cosmic religious" dedication of Einstein, brilliant minds turned to realms of thought seer wisdom had traditionally restricted to closed communities.

Central to the expansion of modern methodological insight is the development of mathematical precision in conjunction with rigorous descriptive analysis. This approach vastly increases the possibility of isolating highly abstract problems and communicating precise answers that resolve them. From high level finance to centralized government and vast military complexes, rational organization aided by computer analysis encourages and rewards growing numbers of methodological seers. Most critical to this methodological surrogate for authentic vision is the twofold transformation of natural philosophy into science and science into technology. Science has grown to become a giant highway for methodological seers. The scientific approach is producing insights so deep and undimensional that they generate human problems of unprecedented gravity. For this reason, it will be helpful to examine one of the most distinguished scientists—Albert Einstein. It is possible that Einstein was a methodological seer.

Einstein is taken here as representative of an ideal type; there is no wish to reduce him by rendering judgment. He is chosen because he generously shared his inner developmental crises with others and also put it in print, but it would be rank presumption to claim to know the entire nature of his inner life—the nature of his soul, so to speak—on this basis. Nevertheless, his life reflects the quality of abstract engagement shared by all seers, but discloses as well the dichotomy between abstract knowledge and humanitarian ideals which racks the modern world. Indeed, the course of his life delineates the depths of frustration and even despair into which the integrity of the seer has fallen.

Einstein's early life is the account of a brilliant young man who succumbed to the pressure for rapid and specialized growth widely encouraged in the modern world. As far as can be discerned from available biographical materials, he achieved individuality by the age of twelve and entered the realm of seer insight within five years. The remaining fifty years of his life were a struggle with the effects of such precocious growth into Spiral VI. When brilliance is driven so early in life to total engagement with a knowledge structure, one forfeits the mature human interrelationships that ripen into free-person self-consciousness and serve as the basis for the true seer. Rapid consolidation of insight was particularly unfortunate in Einstein's case because there were powerful ingredients within his childhood experience that might have produced true seer consciousness. Instead, the course of his life uncovered a dilemma where the regard for human beings carried from childhood never penetrated his early and supreme dedication to "extrapersonal" understanding. He became a great scientist and a respected humanitarian, but respect for humanity did not seem to be the nexus of his absorption in scientific work.

From one point of view, it is surprising that Einstein maintained a vital interest in humanity. As a biographer states, young Einstein "had a constitutional horror of life...this honesty, which made him hesitate to reply to a question until he had thought it over for a long time, seemed to be an anomaly if not a grave defect."[3] Social battering could have led to a wholesale rejection of society if conditions within his family environment had not engendered a deep sense of moral integrity. Einstein's *Autobiographic Notes* state that his first inspiration in life "was religion, which is implanted into every child by way of the traditional educational machine. Thus I came—despite the fact that I was the son of entirely irreligious parents—to a deep religiosity, which, however, found an abrupt ending at the age of 12."[4] Religiosity may have ended, but the warmth and intelligence of an extended Jewish family had provided a sound framework for childhood growth and an enduring sense of humane justice and moral concern.

At twelve, Einstein's growth into individuality was announced by a sweeping condemnation of late nineteenth-century social-adult values: "Even when I was a fairly precocious young man the nothingness of the hopes and striving which chases most men restlessly through life came to my consciousness with considerable vitality. Moreover, I soon discovered the cruelty of that chase, which in those years was much more carefully covered up by hypocrisy and glittering words than is the case today."[5] His rejection of social orientation led to a "positively frantic orgy of freethinking coupled with the impression that youth is intentionally being deceived by the state through lies; it is a crushing impression. Suspicion against every kind of authority grew out of this experience...though later on, because of better insight into causal connections, it lost some of its original poignancy."[6] It is not the justness or accuracy of his criticism that is of immediate interest, but the question as to why his observations—building

from the moral concern established in childhood—did
not lead to a deeper involvement with man's plight. The
quality of seer consciousness was balanced precisely on
this question. Had there been true seer guidance, Einstein's growth into insight might have followed the free-
person sequence already outlined.

A biographer notes that young Einstein read widely
in "the prophets—Moses, Confucious, Buddha, Christ
and the philosophers—Socrates, Aristotle, Spinoza,
Voltaire, Schopenhauer. Most of his excitement, however, came from his books on mathematics, physics
and geometry."[7] Thus he was acquainted with some of
history's greatest seers and free persons. But a passage
from his "Autobiographical Notes" reveals a definite
selectivity in what he absorbed from their collective
vision:

> Out yonder there was this huge world, which exists
> independently of us human beings and which stands
> before us like a great, eternal riddle, at least partially
> accessible to our inspection and thinking. The con-
> templation of this world beckoned like a liberation,
> and I soon noticed that many men whom I had
> learned to esteem and to admire had found inner
> freedom and security in devoted occupation to it.
> The mental grasp of this extrapersonal world within
> the frame of the given possibilities swam half con-
> sciously and half unconsciously before my mind's
> eye. Similarly motivated men of the present and of
> the past, as well as the insights they had achieved
> were the friends which could not be lost.[8]

From these men he did not absorb the plea for self-
transcendence through devotion and compassion for
others. Instead, the great seer message for self-
transcendence served to reinforce engagement with a
nonhuman, extrapersonal world.

The medium for his extrapersonal explorations was, of course, physical science. At seventeen he entered the Polytechnic Institute at Zurich and eight years later, deep in the realm of profound insight, uncovered the interchangeability of matter and energy which led to a reconstitution of thinking about the physical structure of the universe. Over fifty years of deep theoretical probing produced byproducts ranging from nuclear weapons to television tubes and the electron microscope—byproducts that have radically altered the physical circumstances of modern civilization.

Physics was for Einstein much more than an abstractly fascinating endeavor or a means to material prosperity. It was the focus of a relentless pursuit of the "sublimity and marvelous order" he perceived underlying the world of appearance. This "other world" that opens to seer perception is rarely made visible, but with Einstein we are fortunate, for one of the points he made clear about his inner life was the quality of his personal engagement with an extrapersonal world. In addition to the quotation in the last transition, in which Einstein noted that the insight into the mystery of life was coupled with fear, an autobiographical passage composed in 1930 captures the depth of "unconditional" engagement shared by all seers, a depth he aptly characterized as a "cosmic-religious feeling":

> It is very difficult to elucidate this feeling to anyone who is entirely without it, especially as there is no anthropomorphic conception of God corresponding to it.
>
> The individual feels the futility of human desires and aims and the sublimity and marvelous order which reveal themselves both in nature and in the world of thought. Individual existence impresses him as a sort of prison and he wants to experience the

universe as a single significant whole.

The religious geniuses of all ages have been distinguished by this kind of religious feeling, which knows no dogma, and no God conceived in man's image...Looked at in this light, men like Democritus, Francis of Assisi, and Spinoza are closely akin to one another....

In my view, it is the most important function of art and science to awaken this feeling and keep it alive in those who are receptive to it.[9]

This testimony may not reflect the deep joy and human compassion that one finds in Saint Francis. It does reveal the awareness of "sublimity and marvelous order" that lies beyond conditional appearance, an order which cannot be divorced from human nature itself.

With less than five years of individual experience to reorganize, Einstein embraced the vision as an answer to his youthful individuality, even though it was coupled, as he said, with fear. This he accomplished by incorporating his unconditional engagement into a specific science—a process that required extensive probing for what Einstein called fundamentals. Precisely what allows a seer like Einstein to uncover fundamentals within one body of knowledge and not others is as yet unknown. Even when a person is capable of deep insight, considerable preliminary exploration is necessary to isolate the area where operative intuition has its greatest effect. When the depth of probity is as fundamental as it was for Einstein, it often leads the individual insight to sense that the roots of all forms of knowledge are equally deep. Einstein's writing seems impersonal in part because of the language of one particular field, and it sometimes masks his subtlest feelings.

Searching for an area to exercise his powers, Einstein entered the Polytechnic Institute at Zurich with the intention of pursuing both physics and mathematics, but he was obliged to de-emphasize the latter. "This was obviously due," he wrote, "to the fact that my intuition was not strong enough in the field of mathematics in order to differentiate clearly the fundamentally important, that which is really basic, from the rest of the more or less dispensable erudition."[10] Not surprising, inadequate mathematical insight plagued his efforts to elucidate "that which is really basic" in physics, especially when it became clear that "the approach to a more profound knowledge of the basic principles of physics is tied up with the most intricate mathematical methods."[11] In fact, Einstein was a superb mathematician by any ordinary standard, yet inadequate from the seer standpoint, as he himself recognized. Tormented by this problem to his death, among his last words he expressed a wish for "more mathematics."

Understanding the process by which an insight penetrates a body of knowledge to reveal fundamentals would remain quite vague if Einstein had not been vitally concerned with the subject of thinking and its relationship to science. His methodological absorption "in *what* he thinks and how he thinks, not in what he does or what he suffers"[12] is a uniquely valuable source for a provocative look into the complexities of a seer mind. Whether an examination of a Leonardo da Vinci might reveal the same mental processes at work would be difficult to determine. It would appear, however, that Einstein has isolated central factors in Spiral VI perception. His concern with the processes of thinking shows that he recognized the human being primarily as a thinker rather than an emoting or sensing being.

Einstein's elaborate and often obscure analysis of thinking is based on refinements in Kantian epistemology. He begins his analysis of "what and how he thinks" with the functional relationship between sense experience and concepts:

> Out of the multitude of our sense experiences, we take, mentally or arbitrarily, certain repeatedly occurring complexes of sense impression...and we correlate to them a concept—the concept of a bodily object.[13]

In turn, "we attribute to this concept of the bodily object a significance, which is to a high degree independent of the sense impressions which originally gave rise to it."[14]

From this level of conceptualization, systematic knowledge evolves through levels of coherent abstraction. Einstein describes how this process of refinement operates in science:

> Science uses the totality of the primary concepts, i.e., concepts directly connecting them. In its first stage of development, science does not contain anything else. Our everyday thinking is satisfied on the whole with this level. Such a state of affairs cannot, however, satisfy a spirit which is really scientifically minded: because the totality of concepts and relations obtained in this manner is utterly lacking in logical unity. In order to supplement this deficiency, one invents a system poorer in concepts and relations, a system retaining the primary concepts and relations of the "first layer" as logically derived concepts and relations....Further striving for logical unity brings us to a tertiary system, still poorer in concepts and relations, for the deduction of the concepts and relations of the secondary (and so indirectly of the primary) layer. Thus the story goes on until we have arrived at a system of the greatest conceivable unity, and of the greatest poverty of concepts of the logical foundations, which is still compatible with the observations of our senses.[15]

As far as creative insight is concerned, the key is the leap between levels of conceptual abstraction. Fortunately, Einstein was graphically explicit when he stated that the relationship between layers "is not analogous to that of soup to beef, but rather of check number to overcoat."[16] The construction of a systemic body of knowledge is therefore a process of establishing hatchecks for hatchecks until one arrives at an insight like $E=MC^2$, which is enormously abstract but still grounded in the facts of sense experience *through* levels of check numbers.

In reasoning from inclusive insight to particulars, the seer creates new hatchecks by reconstructing layers of conceptual thought, but this is by no means a logical or computerized process. The insightful mind must literally swim through conceptual layers to isolate those concepts intuitively perceived as truly basic. In this selective process, a seer creates his own system of hatchecks or "fundamentals." Fundamentals are then combined and recombined as private hatchecks until a new synthesis is formed. Einstein gave the following explanation of the process which describes both the abstract quality of his creative thought and the complexities of communication after insights crystallize:

> The words of the language, as they are written or spoken, do not seem to play any role in my mechanism of thought. The psychical entities which seem to serve as elements in thought are certain signs and more or less clear images which can be "voluntarily" reproduced and combined.
>
> There is, of course, a certain connection between those elements and relevant logical concepts. It is also clear that the desire to arrive finally at logically connected concepts is the emotional basis of this rather vague play with the above mentioned elements (motor, auditory, visual, and mixed). But taken from a psychological viewpoint, this combinatory play

> seems to be the essential feature in productive
> thought—before there is any connection with logical
> construction in words or other kinds of signs which
> can be communicated to others.... Conventional
> words or other signs have to be sought for labori-
> ously only in a secondary stage, when the mentioned
> associative play is sufficiently established and can be
> reproduced at will.[17]

In the evocative or "primary" stage, the phase *vague
play* means intuitively isolating and combining fundamentals, while *desire* is Einstein's way of expressing
the seer propensity for order, unity, and harmony. Just
as specialized individuals might desire an ordered
life—including a house in the suburbs and a good
car—seers desire insight into cosmic order. The impulse
of the mind is the same in both, the level of operation
differs. Spirals could be characterized in terms of the
level at which coherence is sought.

It is clear from Einstein's description that his productive thought was not spawned in communicable
scientific terminology. In fact "conventional words or
other signs have to be sought for laboriously only in a
secondary stage." Both Teilhard and Einstein record the
communication of insight as an arduous effort. "Maybe
it is inevitable," observed Teilhard while writing *The
Phenomenon of Man*, "maybe it is well, and necessary,
that I should feel at every moment as though I can
advance no further, never sure of the next step."[18] And
Einstein recorded the difficulty of structuring insights
for communication by stating: "I think and I think for
months, for years. Ninety-nine times the conclusion is
false. The hundredth time I am right."[19] The labor involved was captured by Einstein's first wife in reply to
comments by scientists that her husband's insights were
flashes of genius: "Does nobody realize my husband
works himself half to death?"

Through Einstein's account of his inspiration, primary and secondary stages of thought, endless labor and dedication, the awesome realm of seer engagement with unconditional insight comes to focus with rare clarity. And yet, the picture of Einstein's supreme capacity for insight remains incomplete, unintegrated. Consider this statement:

> My passionate sense of social justice and social responsibility was always contrasted oddly with my pronounced lack of need for direct contact with other human beings and human communities. I am truly a "lone traveler" and have never belonged to my country, my home, my friends, or even my family, with my whole heart; in the face of these ties, I have never lost a sense of distance and need for solitude— feelings which increase with the years.[20]

For Einstein, loneliness was a manifestation of estrangement from humanity in the pursuit of his life work. The extent of his alienation is captured by an incident related in Peter Michelmore's biography:

> Once, in the middle of calculations, Ernst Strauss, Einstein's young mathematical assistant at this time, mentioned the Emergency Committee of Atomic Scientists.
> Einstein sighed. "Yes, one must divide his time between politics and equations. But our equations are much more important to me."[21]

The magnitude of methodological seer estrangement from humanity is clearly exposed by Einstein's primary devotion to his equations while fully aware that civilization faced imminent destruction. Einstein represents an individual with Spiral VI consciousness, but not fully integrated with the insights of that spiral. A human being who can be described in terms of Spiral VI is necessarily a loner in that there will be at any time remarkably few people who function on his level. Thus one can imagine a deep love of humanity in the seer coupled with a disinclination to engage many individuals, just as a mother loves children but does not care to handle too many at one time. It may be difficult for most human beings to recognize that they are unknowingly a great strain on the Spiral VI person. A number of stories in the life of Jesus seem to make the same point. Einstein, however, did not fully recognize the inevitability of this position.

The overall impression of Einstein's life presents a brilliant and courageous but troubled and even tragic picture of a lonely man. A giant among men of science, he carried from childhood the time-honored Jewish concern for social justice. This concern was augmented by an awareness of the "marvelous order" underlying the universe and would not allow him to rest at peace in the world of mathematical symbols. He supported the creation of world government, pleaded for the internationalism of atomic energy, and after World War II constantly urged fellow scientists to recognize the need for social responsibility. Nevertheless, he was a victim of the brutal dialectic between individuality and the science that produces methodological seers. Einstein would have been an equally competent scientist had he felt no humanitarian pangs, and he might have led a less troubled life. As it was, his position as intellectual father to thermonuclear energy haunted his later years. He could never resolve the dilemma between his sense of responsibility and the social peril resulting from his scientific work. He could not escape the double nature of the fact that knowledge is power.

The intricacies of seer insight and their effect upon knowledge have been surveyed, but the process through which scientific disciplines encourage methodological orientations also requires attention. As previously stated, sciences are areas of accumulative endeavor through which men as well as ideas grow. Therefore, a science that grows through methodological insight creates a powerful yet subtle methodological syndrome. This syndrome proliferates from allegience to notions like scientific neutrality, dispassionate objectivity, pursuit of truth, and in some cases from the idea of academic freedom. Since the previous inquiry has concentrated upon science, analysis will proceed by examining the notion of "scientific neutrality," although similar conclusions could be derived from considerations of other terms.

In considering scientific neutrality it is helpful to build from Alfred North Whitehead's "fallacy of misplaced concreteness" which labels abstractions fallacious when they become divorced from antecedent sense experience. Scientific thought carefully avoids this pitfall—as demonstrated in Einstein's epistemology—but slips into another fallacy of the same type, a fallacy of misplaced isolation.

Scientific investigation is necessarily founded upon the separation and isolation of variables and constants into identifiable forces, objects, mathematical probabilities, and causal sequences. This activity is quite legitimate. However, the idea of analytical breakdown has become so deeply ingrained in the modern subconscious that a mind-set is produced wherein whole bodies of knowledge are isolated from interacting social realities. Evidence of the mind-set that incorporates misplaced isolation tends to emerge indirectly. It is found, for instance, deep in Einstein's evaluation of scientific thought:

> In guiding us in the creation of such order of sense experience, success alone is the determining factor. All

that is necessary is to fix a set of rules, since without
such rules the acquisition of knowledge in the desired
sense would be impossible. One may compare these
rules with the rules of a game in which, while the
rules themselves are arbitrary, it is their rigidity
alone which makes the game possible. However, the
fixation will never be final.[22]

It is apparent that the idea of "success alone" as the
determining factor in scientific endeavor incorporates a
divorce from social reality. Indeed, mankind may well
cringe in terror at what this idea portends. Moreover,
the quotation embodies an excellent example of misplaced isolation. It is obviously true that epistemic rules
are arbitrary, and analytical rigor is immensely helpful
in isolating fundamentals and communicating insight.
Nonetheless, Einstein misses the point that the *game* (his
term for scientific discipline) is itself arbitrary. Both the
rules and the game are made by man: both are the products of culture-history and both are organically interdependent with society.

The notion of scientific neutrality is an amoral fan-
tasy. There is no separating endeavor from results as
they affect personal and social reality. $E=MC^2$ is not
simply a theoretical formulation exclusively relevant to
the knowledge of physics; it affects the entire structure
of society and the future of all life on earth. The same
is true of all deep insights regardless of the specific
knowledge that nourishes their birth. Philosophically,
the confusion is simple: the rules, guidelines and criteria
governing activity within a sphere of endeavor do not
automatically apply to the sphere as a whole or in its
relation to other spheres.

The consequences of misplaced isolation litter the
landscape of history. In the aftermath of World War II,

Einstein lamented:

> By painful experience we have learned that rational
> thinking does not suffice to solve the problems of our
> social life. Penetrating research and keen scientific
> work have often had tragic implications for
> mankind, producing on the one hand, inventions
> which liberated man from exhausting physical labor,
> making his life easier and richer; but on the other
> hand, introducing a grave restlessness into his life,
> making him a slave to his technological environment,
> and most catastrophic of all—creating the means for
> his own mass destruction. This, indeed, is a tragedy
> of overwhelming poignancy.[23]

Bitterness was added to frustration when Einstein
observed that "the man of science has slipped so much
that he accepts the slavery inflicted upon him by
national states as his inevitable fate. He even degrades
himself to such an extent that he helps obediently in the
perfection of the means for the general destruction of
mankind."[24] Both his observation of the inadequacies of
rationalism and his bitterness are well founded; many
scientists are obediently perfecting the means for general
destruction. But Einstein overlooked the fact that when
science considers itself morally neutral, the results of
scientific insights are inevitably utilized by organizations capable of exploiting their potentialities. In turn,
these organizations exert a powerful influence upon the
course of subsequent research. The crux is that Einstein's
ideas, as well as the services of those scientists he morally deplores, contribute to the syndrome of social
amorality. Moral neutrality within a discipline is based
upon the need to seek without prejudice, and this
requires fearlessness. Moral neutrality outside the
discipline is at best spine-chilling indifference and

irresponsibility, rooted in cowardice.

It is perhaps easier to isolate morality from experimentation in physics than in those sciences concerned with organic life, but even in the latter the deadly drift into moral neutrality is consciously pursued. A statement by the distinguished bacteriologist Rene Dubos clearly pinpoints the trend toward misplaced isolation within the structure of biology:

> Increasingly during recent decades the study of biological problems has been influenced by two large assumptions which at first sight appear to be based on hard-boiled scientific common sense, but in reality are still *sub justice*. One is that life can be understood only by analyzing the mechanisms linking the molecular and animate worlds; the other is that the arrow of influence between these two worlds points in only one direction, from the molecular lifeless components to the more complex patterns of organization found in living things. . . . *They free the scientist from the need to engage in soul-searching about the philosophical meaning of life*, since in the final analysis they equate living processes with the reactions of inanimate matter.[25] (Emphasis added.)

A mind-fix that avoids "soul-searching" will predictably produce both human benefits and human horrors. Recent developments in genetic engineering, for example, have produced beneficial results, but subsequent refinements could lead directly to the dark genetic manipulations prophesied in science fiction novels. If breakthroughs in genetic engineering prove tantamount to $E = MC^2$, society will soon face problems dwarfing even the danger of thermonuclear warfare. And the men of good will who made the breakthroughs will join Einstein in bewildered frustration as the fruits of their labors become socially lethal.

This cycle of moral frustration can be understood in more general terms as a methodological syndrome which corrupts knowledge-structures to eventually plunge society into a series of convulsive reactions. The methodological syndrome begins with an accumulation of particularized knowledge that gives rise to opportunities for growth into methodological insight. In turn methodological insights excite young individuals to strive for Spiral VI consciousness. When a structure becomes powerful through methodological orientation, other structures are provoked to compensate, as for example, when a political or religious structure becomes methodological to cope with military sophistication. In the race that ensues, each methodological structure rapidly expands to become an isolated end in itself— justified by notions like scientific neutrality and political necessity—and the underlying need for compassion toward all men is edged out of the mainstream of knowledge and social activity. At this point people who somehow sense the need for more humane goals form the nucleus of morality movements pressing for revolutionary change. Thus the methodological syndrome includes both increasingly amoral sophistication within structures of human knowledge and a reaction by moral renewal movements striving for revolutionary change within a society. And this syndrome turns upon itself because movements of moral resurgence devoted to revolutionary change easily degenerate into struggles for power. Issues arise, sides are taken, and humane goals are lost as attention is absorbed in the specifics of confrontation. Conflicts have legacies of recrimination and bitterness; preparations are made for the next confrontation; and methodological structures continue to proliferate.

The methodological syndrome can be broken when human endeavor is extracted from amoral isolation, when the exercise of compassion is extricated from confrontations between "we" and "they," when "dispassionate objectivity" becomes "compassionate objectivity," when scientific methodology is no longer synonymous with moral neutrality, and when knowledge is no longer considered an end in itself. Stated previously by many thinkers in diverse ways, the crux bears repetition: *Compassion for others is the only integrative force capable of ordering and harmonizing the flow of evolving life.*

The creation of humane knowledge-structures therefore hinges upon men who incorporate compassion for others into their lifework. In the absence of seer communities organized to confront the growth of amoral knowledge, difficulties in fostering the free-person seer sequence of development assume major proportions. The obvious answer would lie in a renovation of the educational process for the cultivation of free-person consciousness.

It is remarkable that institutional education produces even methodological seers. Consider Einstein's evaluation of his education at Zurich:

> [In physics] I soon learned to scent out that which was able to lead to fundamentals and to turn aside from everything else, from the multitude of things which clutter up the mind and divert it from the essential. The hitch of this was, of course, the fact that one had to cram all this stuff into one's mind for the examinations, whether one likes it or not. This coercion had such a deterring effect [upon me] that, after I had passed the final examination, I found the consideration of any scientific problems distasteful to me for an entire year....It is, in fact, nothing short of a miracle that the modern methods of instruction

> have not entirely strangled the holy curiosity of
> inquiry; for this delicate little plant, aside from
> stimulation, stands mainly in need of freedom;
> without this it goes to wreck and ruin without fail.
> It is a very grave mistake to think that the enjoyment
> of seeing and searching can be prompted by means of
> coercion and a sense of duty."[26]

Einstein further states: "One should never cram young
minds with facts, names and formulae. To know them
you have no need of university courses, you can find
them in books. Education should only be used to teach
young people to think and to give them this training
which no textbook can replace."[27] Coercion and pro-
cedural pressures are certainly rampant in modern
education, but their elimination is not necessarily an
answer for a more humane world. Einstein's formulation of educational requirements, for instance, could be
utilized as a means of creating methodological seers.
One could say that Spiral VI persons emerge despite
their education, not because of it. This is a far cry from
the educational methods proposed by Plato in his
Republic, in which the goal is the maximum actualization of potential in every human being. Plato assumed
that the best for each individual is the best for society
as a whole, a standpoint difficult to recognize below
Spiral V.

Educational philosophy must grapple not only with
coercion but with a range of deep and complex problems
that stretch from infancy to old age. It must encourage
the preparation of individuals ready and capable of
making the leap into freedom. Teachers, students, cur-
riculum, counseling, and institutional factors must be
considered with respect to spirals of awareness. Above
all, education should cultivate the habit of steady concentration, of sustained attention, and should be

directed toward the inborn potential of each student,
for it is in that potential that one finds the power to love
humanity.

If education and psychology hope to encourage the
thorough unfolding of self-consciousness, the problem
of skipped or incomplete spirals of growth should
receive careful attention. In the present study seers who
skip Spiral V were examined in detail because the ex-
igencies they present to the modern world are omnipre-
sent. But similar omissions in self-development are not
at all uncommon, as indicated in Spirals III, IV and V.

Hence it would be a mistake to consider the methodological seer a gross abnormality or "the enemy."
Rather such a person is a profound human tragedy.
He is the analogue to the adult neurotic in Freudian
psychology. Men who should have grown into true
seerdom are instead trapped by both the dimensions of
their responsibilities and an ignorance of the converging
integrity in thoroughly developed self-consciousness.
Yet as human beings they have transcended the ego-
limitations of individuality to develop warmth and
charm, depth and devotion, tenacity and capacity for
grinding work that characterizes all seers. Furthermore,
their capacities quite literally hold together a world
dependent upon rational methodology: were they to
relax their responsibility, war, economic chaos, disease,
and death would rage unrestrained across the world.

Indeed, the pressure of methodological-seer insights is
pushing modern man to a reconsideration of what it
means to be human. At one level of thoughtful concern,
leading world scientists like Niels Bohr, Robert Oppenheimer, and Alexander Sachs have indicated that
what is lacking in our modern world is "not knowledge
of the structure of the universe but a consciousness of
the qualitative uniqueness of human life."[28] There is a
chasm between human self-awareness and knowledge of

our environment, but the dilemma will not be resolved simply by knowing more about ourselves or bridging a gap between knowledge and self-understanding. The solution lies in a reconstitution of understanding itself, a reconstruction based upon total human engagement in self-conscious evolution with all forms of life.

The possibilities for metamorphosis are reasonably clear: the terms of man's engagement with the future are enhanced assimilation and fearless transformation. There can be no rejection of the present by calling forth the old order or starting anew. The future must build from both the depths of the past and the methodological realities of the present. There is no reason why human engagement with the future should be ruled by blindness, nor is it necessary that humanity's deepest insights should continue to imperil life. Comprehensive insight can be grounded in immediate concern for the entire life process rather than the advancement of particular disciplines of knowledge. Ideas need not be thought into history until life harmony has been considered and taken into account.

In pursuing the possibilities inherent in freedom, man has a majestic inheritance from those who have long held in trust the promise of human transcendence. Certainly there are inspiring examples of interacting wisdom. If a small community of Athenian seers—Plato in philosophy, Aeschylus, Sophocles and Euripides in drama, Phydias in sculpture, Ictinus in architecture—could in less than a century lay much of the foundation for Western civilization, what limits are there for interacting wisdom that embraces the entire world?

We cannot measure our debt to those great seers who, like Saint Francis of Assisi, confronted chaos by proclaiming man's splendid engagement with life. Their commitment, inspiring and undeniable, leaps through the ages through missives like Saint Francis' *Song of*

Brother Sun, to proclaim the joyous realities of human freedom:

> Praise to you, my Lord, for all your creatures,
> Above all Brother Sun
> Who brings us the day, and lends us his light;
> Beautiful is he, radiant with great splendor,
> And speaks to us of you, O most high.

> Praise to you, my Lord, for Sister Moon, and for
> the stars;
> In heaven Thou has set them, clear and precious
> and fair.

> Praise to you, my Lord, for Brother Wind,
> For air and clouds, for calm and all weather
> By which they supportest life in all your
> creatures.

> Praise to you, my Lord, for Sister Water
> Which is so helpful and humble, precious and
> pure.

> Praise to you, my Lord, for Brother Fire,
> By whom you light up the night:
> And fair is he, and joyous, and mighty and
> strong.

> Praise to you, my Lord, for our sister, Mother
> Earth,
> Who sustains and directs us,
> And brings forth varied fruits, and plants and
> flowers bright.

> Praise and bless my Lord, and give him thanks,
> And serve him with great humility.[29]

More than pantheism or blind faith, the seer's song reveals the depths of life engagement where the universe is assimilated and enriched to become a masterpiece of self-conscious achievement. The path leading to seerdom begins with the recognition of an inner light and is consummated in the fullness and purity of that light. What might society expect when the penetrating subtlety of an Einstein is wrought with the vision of life unity reflected by a Saint Francis?

Beyond the Seer

One cannot write with any sense of confidence about the possibilities of the human mind beyond Spiral VI. The signs in both Eastern and Western traditions say here is ground instantly corrupted by ignorance and arrogance, here are realms that surpass understanding, here is the "pure light" of indescribable complexity set in a jungle of words with capital letters and systematic contradictions. Perhaps some tentative connections might be made between the possibilities of the mind shared by all men and the qualities of great teachers of compassion (also called Bodhisattvas, Great Ones, Perfected Men, Mahatmas), steeped in continuities beyond ordinary conditions and knowledge. An attempt must be made to link our lives with the possibilities revealed by Gautama Buddha, Jesus of Nazareth, Pythagoras, Krishna, and other omnificent teachers from the near and more distant past. To do so, however, requires a new level of effort. It would be absurd to expect to understand the full range of human potentials without willingness to abandon limited categories, conceptions, notions, and prejudices gained from a lifetime of habit and unexamined experience. With each spiral, the nature of learning and assimilation is altered, and movement beyond Spiral IV is marked by that kind of understanding which cannot be separated from self-transformation. The gaps narrow between knowing and being, thinking and doing (and therefore between epistemology and ethics, science and morality). Growth beyond Spiral VI is signaled by the disappearance of cleavage. John Drinkwater was right to affirm that in worshiping greatness passing by, we ourselves become great; but this alchemy will not occur if we try to bring the great down to our own level. Worship in Drinkwater's sense is a form of aspiration: one rises up toward the level where the object of worship abides. At the minimum, this means that to think of possibilities beyond Spiral VI fruitfully, if tentatively, one must become cosmopolitan in one's perspective—willing to recognize that concepts found in ancient religions and in modern psychology may have merit, that divisions between East and West and between mysticism and science are illusory, and that the promising future of humanity was seen in the oldest philosophical and prophetic traditions. No tribe, race, religion, or national group has preemptive rights to wisdom and understanding, for at the level of wisdom there are no tribes, races, religions, or nationalities.

To summarize the framework for qualitative growth, each spiral from infancy onward represents a system for organizing approximately 10,000 sense impressions per second into a coherent picture of the self and its environment; and each successive spiral incorporates our faculties for perspective within a more abstract and inclusive level of consciousness. Every increase in internal vision is the germ of a wider vision which includes all that came before and also moves into the future. The potential for human consciousness is interminably new, a continuous challenge for more evolved growth. Since the Spiral VI center of orientation is "compassion driven to the roots of knowledge," it is probable that there are more comprehensive realms of understanding beyond the arbitrary and ceaselessly shifting structures of human knowledge.

The final efforts of both Teilhard and Einstein testify to the possibilities of plunging ever deeper into these mental reservoirs that unfold organic interconnections with the past-future continuum of life and energy. Thus Teilhard wrote at the end of his life:

> On the one hand, there is the irresistible confluency of my own individual thought with everything else upon the earth that thinks—and so, closer and closer, with everything that is in the process of "arrangement," wherever it may be, and to whatever degree, in the immensity of time and space.
>
> On the other hand, the continual individualization at the very center of my own little ego, of an ultra-center of thought and action, the irresistible rise, in the depths of my consciousness, of some sort of Other, more me than I am myself.
>
> Thus, we discover, and must acknowledge... a universal flux, bringing unity and irreversibility, in which we are immersed.[30]

The direction beyond Spiral VI is also reflected in Einstein's long search for a unified field theory. As Lincoln Barnett explains:

> In Special Relativity, Einstein demonstrated the equivalence of matter and energy, and in General Relativity he showed the indivisibility of the space-time continuum. His Unified Field Theory sought to culminate and climax this coalescing process....A complete Unified Field Theory touches the "grand aim of all science," which, as Einstein once defined it,

is "to cover the greatest number of empirical facts by logical deduction from the smallest possible number of hypotheses or axioms." The urge to consolidate particularity of the manifest world to the undifferentiated unity that lies beyond is not only the leaven of science, it is the loftiest passion of the human intellect. The philosopher and the mystic, as well as the scientist, have always sought through their various disciplines of introspection to arrive at a knowledge of the ultimate immutable essence that undergirds the mutable illusory world.[31]

It is necessary to comment at length upon the religious and mystical concern with abstract realms of human consciousness. Dante explained the search in the final words of his *Paradiso* as seeking "the lofty light which in Itself is true. Thenceforth my vision was greater than our speech, which yields to such a sight, and the memory yields to such excess." In this vein, Joseph Campbell captured the traditional religious concern with evolving consciousness when he wrote:

Art, literature, myth and cult, philosophy, and ascetic disciplines are instruments to help the individual past his limiting horizons into spheres of ever-expanding realization. As he crosses threshold after threshold, conquering dragon after dragon, the stature of the divinity he summons to his highest wish increases, until it subsumes the cosmos. Finally, the mind breaks the bounding sphere of the cosmos in a realization transcending all experience of form—all symbolizations, all divinities: a realization of the ineluctable void.[32]

Jan van Ruysbroeck spoke of the nude self (the self without self-imposed limitation) ultimately confronting the Nudity, the Divine without attributes. Later in his book *The Hero with a Thousand Faces*, Campbell formulates the fulcrum of these many approaches in the form of a "universal doctrine":

> Briefly formulated, the universal doctrine teaches that all the visible structures of the world—all things and beings—are the effects of a ubiquitous power out of which they rise, which supports and fills them during the period of their manifestation, and back into which they must ultimately dissolve. This is the power known to science as energy, to the Melanesians as *mana*, to the Sioux Indians as *wakonda*, to the Hindus as *Shakti*, and to the Christians as the power of God.[33]

What is implied in the universal doctrine is well known and extremely ancient: the forms of life are ever changing while the substance is changeless; and this substance is, was, and ever will be the same in all things. If the origin is nameless and unknowable, its omnipresence in time is energy, force, will, and love.

It is evident that the human mind is capable of incorporating increasingly abstract centers of orientation. The very abstractness within evolved spirals of growth make conception and direct communication increasingly difficult. High mysticism has been the ultimate response to this difficulty. A passage from Shankara, one of India's greatest seers, echoes hundreds of other commentaries by stating:

> Acting, though not himself the actor; reaping the reward, though not seeking enjoyment; possessing a body, though beyond the body; though hemmed in, yet going everywhere.[34]

Perhaps Western science blended with the psychological subtlety of the East will eventually make frustrated silence unnecessary. Perhaps our understanding of organic continuities, epistemology, energy, and the electromagnetic fields that build the atoms and control the stars will gradually illuminate "mana" for modern man.

The problem of communication may also be responsible for the mystical emphasis on personal withdrawal from worldly concern. Thus the *Bhagavad-Gita* states:

> He whose heart is not attached to objects of sense
> finds pleasure within himself, and through devotion,
> united with the Supreme, enjoys imperishable
> bliss....Such illuminated sages whose sins are ex-
> hausted, who are free from delusion, who have their
> senses and organs under control, and devoted to the
> good of all creatures, obtain assimilation with the
> Supreme Spirit.[35]

Again, Lao-Tzu, the father of Taoism, explained the
way toward perfect enlightenment in terms of withdrawal: "The Way is gained by daily loss, loss upon
loss until at last comes rest. By letting go, it all gets
done; the world is won by those who let it go."[36]
More didactically:

> Stop your senses, close the doors; let sharp things be
> blunted, tangles resolved, the light tempered and tur-
> moil subdued; for this is mystic unity in which the
> Wise Man is moved neither by affection nor yet by
> estrangement or profit or loss or honor or shame.[37]

As consciousness embraces ever more inclusive
centers of orientation, the process of abstraction
necessarily implies liberation from the particularized
concreteness of sense perception. Hence the mind
reaches beyond time and relativity, attraction and
repulsion, subject and object, form and content, joy and
fear, desire and hope, self and God, until it is immersed
in unlocalized or absolute enlightment, Nirvana or absolute consciousness, God or Godhead, Logos or pure
mind, Tao or the Way, Brahma or the Supreme Spirit,
Nous or Divine Spirit. But at this point the question
focuses on whether abstraction means total detachment
from sense perceptions—and here the great religious
traditions have warned against the absorbing bliss that

accompanies absolute enlightenment. As Campbell's extensive study indicates, "there is danger that the bliss of this experience may annihilate all recollection of, interest in, or hope for, the sorrows of this world." He adds by way of elaboration that "the saints are reported to have passed away while in the supernal ecstasy. Numerous indeed are the heroes fabled to have taken up residence in the blessed isle of the unaging Goddess of Immortal Being."[38] Plato called the visionary one who had left the cave of humanity, had seen the Sun, and returned to the cave, and the Buddhists teach that highest Nirvana is samsara, the world of perception.

It is possible that this warning against bliss or "supernal ecstasy" is directed at those who, experiencing an absolute enlightenment, have not consolidated Spiral VI and therefore have not developed the "hatchecks for hatchecks" necessary to anchor levels of abstraction. In any case, it is clear that the approach to absolute enlightenment requires careful preparation:

> The powers of the abyss are not to be challenged lightly. In the Orient, a great point is made of the danger of undertaking the psychologically disturbing practices of yoga without competent supervision. The meditations of the postulate have to be adjusted to his progress, so that the imagination may be defended at every step by *devatas* (envisioned adequate deities) until the moment comes for the prepared spirit to step alone beyond.[39]

Abstractness can mean power to control our internal and external conditions or at least disclose unsuspected potential, as for example when $E=MC^2$ led to the capacity to control nuclear power. Therefore one can reasonably assume that the abstractions which characterize human consciousness beyond seerdom would be enormously powerful. But there we encounter

a profound riddle: what can power mean when consciousness asserts no distinction between power and
purpose, intent and content, cause and effect? Perhaps
this is another way of asking what is the relevance of
growth beyond the seer level—of capacities beyond
ordinary understanding. An indication of the relevance
of these capacities can be gleaned from a statement by
one of the Buddha's favored disciples:

> And now O blessed one,
> Rest beneath the Bodhi tree,
> For thou art the Master of Samadhi.
>
> Behold! thou hast become the light
> Thou hast become the sound,
> Thou art thy Master and thy God,
> Thou art thyself the object of thy search....
>
> And now O Teacher of Compassion,
> Behold those who wait in ignorance and
>   darkness,
> Point thou the way to other men.[40]

Buddha received his enlightenment under the *Bodhi*
(wisdom) tree; and *Samadhi* is the state of unlocalized
or absolute enlightenment. Evidently one must become
the "Master of Samadhi" to enter the Nirvanic field, yet
maintain the control necessary to come and go at will:
"Freedom to pass back and forth across the world divi-
sion, from the perspective of the apparitions of time to
that of the causal deep and back—not contaminating the
principles of the one with those of the other, yet permit-
ting the mind to know the one by virtue of the other—is
the talent of the master."[41] With the ability to pass back
and forth established, "Point the way to other men" can
mean pointing the way to personal enlightenment; and

it can also mean laboring for others by proceeding from an understanding of the primary unity underlying the organic diversity of life on earth. It is difficult to imagine what kind of perspective this represents. Who can assess the importance of ideas like universal brotherhood, forgiveness of injury, and boundless compassion through centuries of internecine warfare? Who can measure the impact of statements such as "the light that lighteth every man that cometh into the world," or "let the sins of the world fall upon me that I may relieve man's misery and suffering?" Who could challenge the effects of persistent gentleness that calls for humility and love in the midst of violence and despair? This much is clear: those who have not shared the experiences of Spiral VI dare not prejudge the potency of such forces any more than a two-year-old who has just learned the language can dare to judge the power of poetry.

The significance of such questions cannot be considered without coming to terms with their relevance to the individual and the community. Many otherwise sincere people run afoul of the question of happiness, that bugbear of contemporary psychology and the perennial problem of philosophy. As long as one insists on seeing happiness, contentment, satisfaction or fulfillment in personal terms, one cannot even begin to understand the fundamentals of human nature. Many humble individuals have come to the profound truth that suffering is a great teacher, not because pain is knowledge, but because it induces self-questioning. When self-questioning is not made a natural part of one's life, concretized and insupportable notions of personal happiness prevent further growth. Secure happiness and self-fulfillment are to be found by inserting oneself into the larger picture that embraces oneself with the whole of life. As pointed out by Raghavan Iyer in *Parapolitics*, self-transcendence means "self-forgetfulness."[42]

As is obvious in children who enjoy learning new skills and who enthusiastically emulate adults, growth through the spirals occurs only when one *wants to grow*. Nature and circumstances can only force us so far and no further; we have to cooperate with nature. While this study has examined blocks to growth, it has not looked at perversity, the willful refusal to grow. Failure to transcend limits is easier to understand than the urge for some form of self-destruction. Such willful tendencies have been judged as outside the scope of this work. The following succinct expression by Iyer is intended for those open to normal growth:

> There is, in fact, no substitute either for the philosophical task of confronting alternative propositions or for the practical endeavor of singling out visible examples of maturity in the quest for self-awareness.[43]

As the child looks to those who embody the qualities they lack, the adult must be willing to examine all things. In this, young people sometimes do better than their elders who have a vested interest in pretending to have come to terms with the riddles of life. Many have shown a remarkable freedom from prejudices inherited from the nineteenth century when they turned to Mahatma Gandhi for guidance. He wrote, "I ask nobody to follow me. Everyone should follow his or her own inner voice." Yet within the sublime tolerance for every shade of opinion and a vast variety of outlooks, he showed millions of people that one does not have to accept the "rules of the game" or the presuppositions of any system to be an effective participant in society while maintaining the highest integrity.

He converted a passive principle of meek submission

to evil and injustice into a dynamic doctrine of non-
violent activity in the cause of truth and justice, a
universal commandment to exercise the power of
love and compassion on the basis of inner strength,
not outer weakness.[44]

The fact that young people study, respond to, and
assimilate the thought and principles of a man with
Gandhi's wisdom and compassion suggests that we live
in an age of transition that holds great promise for the
future. Perhaps Margaret Mead was right in suggesting
that we are moving into a historical epoch in which the
old learn from the young rather than the reverse, traditional mode. In a transitional age it is important to have
self-chosen exemplars to emulate, but it is even more
important to confront broad philosophical questions.
Many people who fully recognize the importance of
confronting psychological realities do not see the value
of experimenting with philosophical perspectives. When
one thinks of the suffering and slaughter perpetrated
and perpetuated in the name of religious dogma and
philosophical doctrine, the view that philosophical
questions are irrelevant becomes a tragic illusion.

Many deeply feel the need to ask questions and explore alternatives, and they often engage in activities of
the kind surveyed in Marilyn Ferguson's *The Aquarian
Conspiracy* (a study of personal and social transformation in the 1980s). The immediacy of the kinds of inquiry delineated here should not blind us to the fact that
most efforts to question result in shuffling data and
categories whose usefulness has already been exhausted.
Enduring insights and authentic answers cannot be
found in Spiral IV activity. Even common talk of the ad-
vent of the "Aquarian Age," cast in terms of newspaper
astrology and sociological jargon, is little more than an
index of the depth of need for serious rethinking of

human nature, community, and the future of mankind. Nevertheless, current ferment in all areas of life does reflect the dawn of vital changes in humanity. The logic of spirals of consciousness implies that what is true of individuals is also true of humanity as a whole, though over a vast period of time far outdistancing the epoch called recorded history and perhaps even the dates given by paleontologists and anthropologists. Furthermore, when we consider that the spirals of consciousness constitute a model illustrated by ideal types, and the fact that human beings are marvelously complex, we see that most of us participate in several spirals simultaneously. Even while a person is striving for self-definition as an individual, there is that in him or her which yearns to transcend the limitations of individuality. In raising these philosophical questions, universal frameworks are needed.

Such frameworks have always existed, as Einstein knew, in the great philosophical and religious traditions that constitute the common inheritance of humanity. Collectively we contain all the spirals at any given time, making evolution possible, and the highest perspective can be found in the most contemporary thinking. The hallmark of such thinking is that it raises us out of our habitual modes of thought while at the same time it is applicable to each human being in any spiral or phase of life. "Aquarian thinking"—if we are to give authentic significance to the term—closes the rent between thought and action (idea and performance) so that our lives are woven as seamless fabric.

Hence we should be able to gain a more rounded picture of ourselves and the world and as the world becomes truly whole we will begin to blossom:

> As one acquires a more universal perspective in relation to the masks of time—memory and desire, regret

and anticipation, and the irrational fears that consolidate the shadow—they fall away and one's eyes
are opened to the noumenal light of the invisible
world....Through daily practice one experiences a
deeper kinship with all that lives and breathes, a
greater love of other human beings, a truer realization of the cosmic Self, a profounder conviction of
universal brotherhood.[45]

Beginning to live in terms of such a vision restores
human dignity, the sense in which each human being
has a destiny, a sense that becomes as powerful as it is
undramatic and unpretentious. To reach beyond Spiral
VI is to dispel all illusions and know no difference between oneself and the whole of cosmic life. It is to make
the plan of nature the very framework of our own being
and the deliberate basis for one's outlook on life. By the
laws of dialectic, growth beyond Spiral VI would involve a synthesis between wisdom and compassion, a
movement from the transpersonal to the transhuman
realm beyond all categories of thought. No concept of
the immensity of infinity can capture the boundlessness
of invisible space, eternal duration, or unqualified consciousness. This can only be experienced at the deepest
level where the whole of one's being is alive and awake.
When asked who he was, Gautama simply replied,
"I am Buddha," literally, "I am awake."

Each person is in principle aware of boundless space,
ceaseless motion, and eternal duration—qualities
beyond the realm of opposites. One can always draw
the larger circle, can always accommodate all points and
make them compatible in terms of something higher or
more inclusive. Humanity therefore should have the
potential to evolve beyond all possible modes of
manifestation to simultaneously embrace the one in the
many and the many in the one—to unveil an inmost

center that is truly free. Socially, that inmost center is the root of all human evolution, a perpetual source of promise, potential, and collective progress. Individually, the highest vision must be equivalent to unqualified human freedom, emancipation from all conditions of consciousness, symbolized in the ancient Hindu texts by *Soma*, the elixir of self-regeneration.

> Even in the dawn of the Aquarian Age, some forerunners may be entitled to exclaim: "We have drunk *Soma*, we have become immortal, we have entered into light, we have known the gods."[46]

Notes

Introduction

1. Lecomte Du Nouy, *Human Destiny*, (New York: Longmans, Green and Company, 1947), pp. 10-11.

2. Joseph Pearce, *Magical Child* (New York: Bantam Books, 1980), p. 33.

3. See *Magical Child*, pp. 6-9.

Spiral I

1. Erik H. Erikson, "Identity and the Life Cycle," *Psychological Issues* (New York: International Universities Press, Inc., 1959), vol. 1, no. 1, p. 63.

2. Erikson, Ibid., p. 69.

3. The material on Piaget is taken from Henry W. Maier, *Three Theories of Child Development*, (New York: Harper and Row, 1978).

Spiral II

1. Erikson, "Identity and Life Cycle," p. 113.

2. Ibid., p. 74.

3. Ibid., p. 7.

4. Lawrence Kohlberg, "Development of Moral Character and Moral Ideology," *Review of Child Development Research* (New York: Sage, 1964), p. 400.

5. Ibid., p. 104.

6. Erikson, "Identity and Life Cycle," p. 92.

7. A challenging analysis of the effects produced by the modern media of communication is presented in Marshall McLuhan's *Understanding Media: The Extensions of Man* (New York: New American Library, 1973).

8. Erikson, "Identity and Life Cycle," p. 113.

9. Ibid., pp. 115-16.

Spiral III

1. Erikson, "Identity and Life Cycle," pp. 118 and 113.

2. This brief survey of the infantile-adult is distilled from a variety of sources that center in the problem of alienation and identity in modern society. For background material, see Erik and Mary Josephson, eds., *Man Alone*; Stein, Vidich, and White eds., *Identity and Anxiety*; C. G. Jung, *The Undiscovered Self*; Erik Erikson, *Childhood and Society*; Viktor Frankl, *Man's Search for Meaning*; Erich Fromm, *Beyond the Chains of Illusion*.

3. E. F. Schumacher, *A Guide for the Perplexed* (New York: Harper and Row, 1978).

4. Albert Camus, *The Stranger*, tr. Gilbert Stuart (New York: Vintage Books, Inc., 1954), pp. 151, 154.

5. Albert Camus, *The Rebel*, tr. Anthony Bower (New York: Vintage Books, Inc., 1956), p. 306.

6. Frederick Weiss, "Self-Alienation: Dynamics and Therapy." In Eric and Mary Josephson, *Man Alone*, (New York: Dell Publishing Co., 1975), p. 447.

7. Richard Wilhelm and C. G. Jung, *The Secret of the Golden Flower*, (New York: Causeway Books, 1975), p. 88.

8. Daniel J. Levinson, *The Seasons of a Man's Life* (New York: Ballantine Books, 1979), pp. 198-199.

9. Ibid., p. 26.

10. Peter Berger, *Invitation to Sociology* (New York: Viking, Overlook Press, 1973), pp. 74-75.

11. Erik Erikson, *Childhood and Society* (New York: W. W. Norton and Co., Inc., 1975), pp. 279 and 282.

12. Levinson, *Seasons*, p. 243.

Spiral IV

1. Gail Sheehy, *Passages* (New York: Bantam Books, 1981), p. 18.

2. Lawrence Kohlberg, *The Philosophy of·Moral Development* (San Francisco: Harper & Row, 1981), pp. 344-345.

3. Dwight Goddard, *A Buddhist Bible* (Boston: Beacon Press, 1970), p. 356.

4. Leo Tolstoy, in William James, *The Varieties of Religious Experience* (Garden City, N.Y. Doubleday, Image Books, 1978), pp. 161-63 and 191-92.

5. Claude Cuenot, *Teilhard de Chardin* (Baltimore: Helicon Press, Inc., 1965), p. 373.

6. E. M. Abrahamson and A. W. Pezet, *Body, Mind and Sugar* (New York: Pyramid Books, 1971), p. 170.

7. j. Bronowski, *The Western Intellectual Tradition* (New York: Harper Torchbooks, 1962), p. 283.

8. Arthur Koestler, *Darkness at Noon* (New York: Signet Classics, 1961), p. xiv.

9. Erikson's counterparts are "basic trust vs. mistrust, autonomy vs. doubt, initiative vs. guilt, industry vs. inferiority, identity vs. role diffusion, intimacy vs. isolation, generativity vs. stagnation, and ego integrity vs. despair."

10. Lewis Mumford, *The Transformations of Man* (Gloucester, Mass.: Peter Smith, 1978), p. 138.

Spiral V

1. Kohlberg, "Development of Moral Character," (see n. 4, Spiral II), p. 401.

2. Teilhard de Chardin, *The Phenomenon of Man* (New York: Harper Colophon, 1975), p. 263.

3. G. W. F. Hegel, *Reason in History* (New York: Bobbs-Merrill Co., Inc., 1953), p. 25.

4. Abraham Maslow, *Toward a Psychology of Being* (New York: D. Van Nostrand Co., Inc., 1968), pp. 137-141.

5. Ibid.

6. Ibid., p. 96.

7. Ibid., p. 114.

8. Ibid., p. 163.

9. Erikson, *Childhood and Society*, p. 52.

10. C. G. Jung, *Archetypes and the Collective Unconscious*, tr. R. F. C. Hull (Princeton: Princeton University Press, Bollingen Series XX, 1977), p. 287.

11. Teilhard de Chardin, *Phenomenon of Man*, p. 33.

12. *The Atlantic*, August, 1966, published an article drawn from material presented at the Albert Schweitzer International Convocation at Aspen, Colorado, 1966, one year after Schweitzer's death.

13. Albert Einstein, "Autobiographical Notes," in Paul Schlipp, ed., *Albert Einstein* (New York: Harper Torchbooks, 1959), vol. 1, p. 53.

14. Henri Michaux, *Light Through Darkness* (London: Bodley Head Ltd., 1964), pp. 177-78.

15. W. Y. Evans-Wentz, *The Tibetan Book of the Great Liberation* (London: Oxford University Press, 1980), p. 226.

16. Joseph Campbell, *The Hero with a Thousand Faces* (New York: Bollingen Series XVII, 1973), pp. 354-355.

17. Albert Einstein, *Living Philosophies* (New York: Simon and Schuster, Inc., 1931), pp. 6-7.

18. All statements by Allen Ginsberg are from *Life Magazine*, May 27, 1966.

19. Lucien Goldmann, *The Hidden God*, tr. Philip Thody (New York: Humanities Press, 1964), p. 171.

20. Ibid., p. 60.

21. Ibid., pp. 229-30.

22. Interestingly, Bergson himself is a transitional philosopher who attempted to resolve a number of conflicts.

23. Henri de Lubac, *Teilhard de Chardin* (New York: Hawthorne Books, Inc., 1965). Also see l'abbe Paul Grenet, *Teilhard de Chardin: The Man and His Theories*, tr. R. A. Rudorff (New York: Paul Erikson, Inc., 1965), p. 59.

24. Teilhard de Chardin, "Christ in Matter," in Neville Braybrooke, ed., *Teilhard de Chardin: Pilgrim of the Future* (New York: Seabury Press, Inc., 1965), pp. 18-19.

25. Teilhard de Chardin, *The Making of a Mind* (New York: Harper and Row, Inc., 1965), p. 271.

26. Ibid., p. 268.

27. Cuenot, *Teilhard de Chardin* (see n. 5, Spiral IV), p. 71.

28. Grenet, *Teilhard de Chardin*, p. 96.

29. Ibid., p. 118.

30. Teilhard de Chardin, *Letters from a Traveller* (London: Collins Co. Ltd., 1962), pp. 207, 209.

31. Lucille Swan, "Memories and Letters," in Braybrooke, ed., *Teilhard de Chardin*, p. 46.

32. Ibid., p. 45.

33. Cuenot, *Teilhard*, p. 362.

34. See Sir Julian Huxley's introduction to *The Phenomenon of Man*, pp. 24-25.

Spiral VI

1. The only comprehensive descriptive analysis of ancient seership is in *The Cult of the Seer in the Ancient Middle East*, by Violet MacDermot (University of California Press, Berkeley, 1971). However, this discussion does not deal with the seer as a state of consciousness that can be cultivated through a lifelong discipline, as recognized in Buddhist schools of meditation and Hindu teachings on Raja Yoga.

2. Raghavan Iyer, *Parapolitics* (New York: Oxford University Press, 1979), p. 360.

3. Hilaire Cuny, *Albert Einstein* (New York: Paul S. Erikson, Inc., 1965), p. 16.

4. Albert Einstein, "Autobiographic Notes," in Paul Schlipp, ed., *Albert Einstein: Philosopher-Scientist* (New York: Harper Torchbooks, 1959), vol. 1, pp. 3-5.

5. Ibid., p. 3.

6. Ibid., p. 5.

7. Peter Michelmore, *Einstein, Profile of the Man* (New York: Dodd, Mead & Co., 1962), p. 30.

8. Einstein, "Autobiographic Notes," p. 5.

9. *New York Times Magazine*, November 9, 1930, pp. 2-3.

10. Einstein, "Autobiographical Notes," p. 15.

11. Ibid., p. 17.

12. Ibid., p. 33.

13. Albert Einstein, "Physics and Reality," *The Journal of the Franklin Institute*, vol. 221, no. 3, March, 1936.

14. Ibid.

15. Ibid.

16. Ibid.

17. Albert Einstein, "Letter to Jacques Hadamard," in Brewster Ghiselin, ed., *The Creative Process* (New York: Mentor Books, 1957), p. 43.

18. De Lubac, *Einstein*, p. 83.

19. Michelmore, *Einstein*, p. 171.

20. Einstein, "Letter to Jacques Hadamard," p. 9.

21. Michelmore, *Einstein*, p. 238.

22. Einstein, "Physics and Reality."

23. Cuny, *Einstein*, p. 157.

24. Einstein, "Letters to Jacques Hadamard," p. 358.

25. René Dubos, *The Dreams of Reason* (New York: Columbia University Press, 1961), p. 115.

26. Einstein, "Letters to Jacques Hadamard," p. 17.

27. Cuny, *Einstein*, p. 161.

28. Mumford, *Transformations* (see n. 10, Spiral IV), p. 92.

29. Saint Francis of Assisi, "Song of Brother Sun," in C. W. Hollister, *Medieval Europe* (New York: John Wiley & Sons, Inc., 1982), p. 212.

30. Cuenot, *Teilhard*, p. 371.

31. Lincoln Barnett, *The Universe and Dr. Einstein* (New York: Bantam Books, 1978), p. 113-114.

32. Campbell, *Hero with a Thousand Faces*, pp. 257-58.

33. Ibid., p. 258.

34. Shankaracharya, *Vivekachudamani*.

35. *The Bhagavad-Gita*, Chapter V.

36. Lao-Tzu, *The Way of Life*, tr. R. B. Blakney (New York: Mentor Books, Inc., 1964), p. 101.

37. Ibid., p. 109.

38. Campbell, *Hero with a Thousand Faces*, p. 193.

39. Ibid., pp. 201-2.

40. Rephrased from *The Voice of the Silence* (Wheaton, Ill.: Theosophical Publishing House, Quest Books, 1980), pp. 34-35.

41. Campbell, *Hero with a Thousand Faces*, p. 229.

42. Iyer, *Parapolitics*, p. 103.

43. Ibid., p. 110.

44. Raghavan N. Iyer, *The Moral and Political Thought of Mahatma Gandhi* (New York: Oxford University Press, 1973), p. 215. The quotation from Gandhi is also cited on this page.

45. "The Pilgrimage of Humanity," *Hermes*, Vol. VI, no. 8 (1980), pp. 342-343.

46. "The Aquarian Elixir," *Hermes*, Vol. VIII, no. 9 (1982), p. 398.

Selected Bibliography

Barnett, Lincoln. *The Universe and Dr. Einstein*. New York: Bantam Books, 1978.

Besant, Annie, trans., *The Bhagavad Gita*. Wheaton, Il.: Theosophical Publishing House, 1974.

Blavatsky, H. P. *The Voice of the Silence*. Wheaton, Il.: Theosophical Publishing House, 1973.

Bronowski, J. *The Western Intellectual Tradition*. New York: Harper Torchbooks, 1962.

Campbell, Joseph. *The Hero with a Thousand Faces*. Princeton: Princeton University Press, Bollingen Series, XVII, 1973.

Camus, Albert. *The Rebel*. New York: Vintage Books, Inc., 1956.

_____. *The Stranger*. New York: Vintage Books, Inc., 1954.

Einstein, Albert. *Ideas and Opinions*. New York: Dell Publishers, 1978.

Erikson, Erik. *Childhood and Society*. New York: Norton, 1975.

Evans-Wentz, W. Y. *The Tibetan Book of the Great Liberation*. London: Oxford University Press, 1980.

166

Ferguson, Marilyn. *The Aquarian Conspiracy*. Boston: Houghton Mifflin Co., 1980.

Frankl, Viktor. *Man's Search for Meaning*. New York: Pocket Books, 1976.

Fromm, Erich, D. T. Suzuki, Richard DeMartino. *Zen Buddhism and Psychoanalysis*. New York: Harper Colophon Books, 1970.

Goddard, D. *A Buddhist Bible*. Boston: Beacon Press, 1970.

Hermes. Concord Grove Press. P.O. Box 959. Santa Barbara, Ca. 93102

Hollister, C. W. *Medieval Europe*. New York: John Wiley and Sons, 1982.

Iyer, Raghavan, ed. *The Jewel in the Lotus*. Santa Barbara: Concord Grove Press, 1983.

————. *The Moral and Political Thought of Mahatma Gandhi*. Santa Barbara, Ca.: Concord Grove Press, 1983.

————. *Parapolitics: Toward the City of Man*. Santa Barbara, Ca.: Concord Grove Press, 1983.

James, William. *The Varieties of Religious Experience*. New York: Viking Penguin, 1982.

Jung, C. G. *Memories, Dreams, Reflections*. New York: Vintage Books, 1965.

————. *The Undiscovered Self*. New York: Mentor Books, 1964.

Kohlberg, Lawrence. *The Philosophy of Moral Development*. San Francisco: Harper and Row, 1981.

Lao-Tzu. *The Way of Life*, trans. by R. B. Blakney. New York: Mentor Books, 1964.

Levinson, D. J. *The Seasons of a Man's Life*. New York: Ballantine Books, 1979.

Mumford, Lewis. *The Transformations of Man*. New York: Glouster, Mass.: Peter Smith, 1978.

Piaget, Jean. *The Child and Reality*. New York: Grossman Publishers, 1973.

Schlipp, Paul, éd. *Albert Einstein: Philosopher-Scientist*. New York: Harper Torchbooks, 1959.

Schumacher, E. F. *A Guide for the Perplexed*. New York: Harper and Row, 1977.

Sheehy, Gail. *Passages*. New York: Bantam Books, 1981.

Stace, W. T. *The Teachings of the Mystics*. New York: Mentor Books, 1960.

Teilhard de Chardin, Pierre. *The Phenomenon of Man*. New York: Harper Colophon, 1975.